IMAGES
of America

LATINOS IN THE WASHINGTON METRO AREA

This 1819 map shows the Washington metro area before the many waves of national and international peoples, including Latinos, came to make it their home. The area includes the federal district and parts of Maryland and Virginia. Over time, Latinos have built communities throughout the area and have made Washington, DC, a livelier and a culturally richer place to live. (Courtesy of the Library of Congress, Geography and Map Division.)

On the Cover: Shortly after emigrating from Paraguay to Washington, DC, in 1966, dance teacher Celia Ruiz Dominguez (pictured on the far right) assembled a dance troupe to showcase traditional Paraguayan dances and integrate Paraguayan culture into the lives of her children and those in her community. Professor Dominguez choreographed the traditional *polca* dances, a genre that evolved from European dances and was introduced to Paraguay in the 1800s and is the official national music and dance of Paraguay. This picture was taken in 1969. (Courtesy of Ana Maria Serafini.)

IMAGES *of America*

LATINOS IN THE WASHINGTON METRO AREA

Maria Sprehn-Malagón,
Jorge Hernandez-Fujigaki,
and Linda Robinson

ISBN 978-1-5316-7322-2

Published by Arcadia Publishing
Charleston, South Carolina

Library of Congress Control Number: 2013952365

For all general information, please contact Arcadia Publishing:
Telephone 843-853-2070
Fax 843-853-0044
E-mail sales@arcadiapublishing.com
For customer service and orders:
Toll-Free 1-888-313-2665

Visit us on the Internet at www.arcadiapublishing.com

To Javier, Helena, and Maria Helena Malagón, and to Alba Robinson—their enthusiasm and appreciation of Hispanic culture and community spans generations. And to Claudia, for always being there.

Contents

Acknowledgments

We are extremely grateful to Olivia Cadaval, who generously shared her knowledge, pictures, and stories of the Latino community launching us on a project that was difficult to stop. Photographers Rick Reinhard, Michael Hoyt, and Sam Corum kindly contributed their storytelling pictures. Paula Andalo of *El Tiempo Latino* and Miguel Vivanco of *El Pregonero* graciously supplied numerous photographs and tips for telling this story. We are truly appreciative of all the contributors who searched through their attics, basements, closets, hidden boxes, and albums to find the snapshots that make this story come to life. And finally, we are thankful to Isabel and Maria Elisa Lamporte, third-generation Spaniards, who have shown remarkable patience during this project.

INTRODUCTION

This collection of pictures offers only a glimpse into the rich history and culture of the Washington, DC, area's Latino community, mostly before the advent of digital photography. The challenge of constructing this snapshot of Latino life was locating the stored pre-digital photographs in a world dominated by electronic files. The greater challenge, however, was stopping the process of collecting the stories and photographs. As more people contributed their stories and photographs, the more interesting this story became. Hopefully this small compilation of images will complement current projects, lead to future inquiries, and perhaps inspire more people to share their stories and pictures with one another and preserve them for future generations.

The Hispanic presence in the Washington, DC, area has historical depth and diverse roots. This area has been a destination for and influenced by travelers and immigrants of the Hispanic diaspora since the 16th century. The earlier visitors to and residents of the region were small in number, though they represented many different countries and cultures of origin. It was not until the late 20th century that the number of Hispanic residents in the area increased dramatically. This rise in the Latino population resulted in the formation of new communities that share an immigrant experience and broad cultural ties. It has also created new forms of cultural expression and identity. Some of the photographs in this book predate the use of the terms *Hispanic* and *Latino*, which are recent categories. The US Census first used the term *Hispanic* in 1980. In this book, the terms refer to people who have ancestry and cultural ties to Latin America and the Iberian Peninsula.

The Latino community in the Washington, DC, metro area today is the 12th largest in the nation. It is unique in that no single ethnic group forms a majority. Although Salvadorans form the largest group, this area is also home to those who hail from Mexico, Puerto Rico, Guatemala, Cuba, Dominican Republic, Bolivia, Argentina, Chile, Colombia, Ecuador, Honduras, Nicaragua, Paraguay, Peru, Spain, Uruguay, and many other nations and cultures. This area also has the largest Bolivian community, the highest number of Latino college graduates, and one of the highest standards of living for Latinos in the United States.

As a national capital, Washington, DC, has drawn residents from throughout the world. These residents made and continue to make the metro area extremely diverse. The earlier Hispanic residents were comprised of diplomats and professionals working at embassies and other international institutions and organizations. They were often accompanied by staff and domestic workers who sometimes stayed in the area while their employers moved on to new posts. It was not unusual for the children of international employees as well as those of their domestic workers to stay in this area and become first-generation Latinos.

The earlier arrivals were less visible than the immigrants who arrived in the 1980s and onward in greater numbers. Fortunately, the pre-1980 arrivals are visible in the photographic record, made up mostly of family and personal albums showing how they forged communities and became Washingtonians, Marylanders, and Virginians. Puerto Rican and Mexican-American white-collar professionals who were already citizens came to the DC area looking for federal jobs linked to the New Deal and World War II in the 1930s and 1940s. In the late 1950s and early 1960s, in response to revolution and political upheaval, many Cuban and Dominican immigrants arrived in the area. Soon after, during the 1960s and 1970s, many South Americans arrived, escaping the conflicts and crises in their countries.

The early residents generated a demand for Latino businesses and services, such as restaurants and markets that provided an economic base for other Latino immigrants and created a foundation for the diverse Latino community of today. Some of the earlier Latino businesses mentioned in works by Olivia Cadaval and Elaine Peña are several DC markets, including Casa Peña, which existed in the 1950s; Casa Diloné, a Dominican market; La Sevillana; and the Panamerican Laundry. The Churreria Madrid, a restaurant that serves churros (which taste like a Spanish version of funnel cake) and Spanish dishes, opened in 1973 in Adams Morgan. By mid-century, there were church services being conducted in Spanish. In Washington, DC, St. Paul's Church and the Church of the Sacred Heart offered Spanish-language services, and in Potomac, Maryland, the chapel of the Academy of American Franciscan History did as well.

The earlier arrivals also started public celebrations, such as the Latino Festival, which still occur in DC. In her book, *Creating a Latino Identity in the Nation's Capital: The Latino Festival*, Olivia Cadaval traces the history of this festival since its beginning in 1970. In more recent times, Latinos moved to the suburbs and nearby cities, and more Latino festivals have emerged. Baltimore has been celebrating a Latino Festival for 33 years, and the city of Frederick has for 9 years.

During the 1980s and 1990s, the armed conflicts of El Salvador, Guatemala, Honduras, and Nicaragua brought many immigrants from these countries to the Washington, DC, area. The earlier migrations of women from Central America who came to the region, working as domestic workers for diplomats and families working at the international institutions, carved the path for the arrival of many who were fleeing the conflicts. As a result of these original arrivals, a process of chain migration that brought relatives and friends began in the 1980s. As noted by Lopez and Dockterman (2012: 88), almost half (46 percent) of today's Washington, DC, metro area Hispanics are from or trace their ancestry to Central American countries.

The substantial demographic increase of Latinos in the 1980s and 1990s transformed the DC area to a place where the Spanish language is common and the people and culture of the Iberian diaspora form a prominent part of the area's identity. Latinos work and are successful in all occupational positions and contribute to politics, education, and the arts. They have contributed to creating the community organizations that today continue to assist newly arrived immigrants and to the schools that have established language programs for children. Today, through the work of many Latinos, adult immigrants can learn English and pursue training for more skilled positions. The once exotic and unknown dishes and foods from Latin America and the Iberian Peninsula are more easily found and have been mainstreamed, requiring little or no explanation for non-Latinos. Few people in the area knew what a *pupusa* was until the 1980s. Today, supermarkets have Hispanic food aisles and votive candles for the numerous patron saints of the Hispanic diaspora. Families have blended. The newer and the older immigrants, Latino and other, have shared in creating a culturally richer and livelier Washington metro area.

One

The Beginnings

Before the establishment of continuous English settlements in the mid-Atlantic region, Spanish and Portuguese explorers sailed into the waters today known for weekend and summer escapes for metro-area residents. These Iberian explorers provided the first descriptions of the area. In 1525, while exploring the possibility of a passage to the Pacific for the Spanish Crown, Portuguese-born Esteban Gomez sailed into the Chesapeake Bay. His ship harbored near today's White Haven, Maryland. Lucas Vásquez de Ayllón, Juan Menéndez Marqués, Juan Lara, Vicente González, Francisco Fernández Ecija, and others also explored and reported on what are today the Chesapeake Bay and its surroundings.

Following independence from Spain and Portugal, mostly during the early and mid-1800s, Latin American countries established diplomatic relations with the United States. First called legations, these diplomatic missions later became embassies. Symbolic of these early relationships with Latin American countries are the many monuments and buildings throughout the city. Some examples include the Columbus Fountain in front of Union Station and, on main avenues and public places, the many statues of Latin American historical figures, including José Gervasio Artigas (Uruguay), Simón Bolivar (Venezuela), José de San Martín (Argentina), Bernardo de Gálvez (Spain), and Benito Juarez (Mexico). These were gifts from these countries to the United States.

Also notable is the Hispanic Reading Room at the Library of Congress. This division of the Library of Congress began in 1927 with donations from Archer M. Huntington, the founder of the Hispanic Society of America, which is headquartered in New York. In 1939, the Hispanic Division and the Hispanic Reading Room were created for Spanish and Portuguese acquisitions.

Today, the early presence of Hispanic peoples in the area is noted in the architecture, sculpture, art, and object collections of many institutions. Late-19th-century and early-20th-century photographs provide glimpses of some of the people who were part of the community that made these contributions. The legations, visitors, and residents who came to Washington, DC, during this early period set the stage for the arrival of many others in the following century.

This section of a 1562 map by Spanish cartographer Diego Gutiérrez and Dutch engraver Hieronymus Cock shows the Atlantic coastline. The Bajía de Santa Maria, just northwest of the stylized fish, is today called the Chesapeake Bay. Iberian explorers visited the Chesapeake Bay and its surroundings during the 16th and 17th centuries, providing the first descriptions of the area. (Courtesy of the Library of Congress.)

David Glasgow Farragut (1801–1870), a second-generation Spaniard in the United States, resided in Washington, DC, attended the US Naval Academy, and played an important role in the American Civil War. His father was Jorge Farragut of Menorca, Spain, who came to the Americas and fought against the British in the Revolutionary War. (Courtesy of the Library of Congress.)

At the residence of the Brazilian Legation in Washington, DC, Madame Mendonça is seated in her boudoir. She is the wife of Salvador Furtado de Mendonça Drummond, envoy extraordinary and minister plenipotentiary from Brazil to the United States. The picture is dated 1893. (Courtesy of the Library of Congress.)

The First Pan American Financial Conference was held in Washington, DC, in May 1915. This image shows, from left to right, the Argentine minister Rómulo Sebastián Naón, Maria Teresa Quintana Pearson, Isabel Pearson Quintana, and Samuel Hale Pearson, an Argentine official during the conference. (Courtesy of the Library of Congress.)

This January 13, 1920, picture shows the technical advisor of the Brazilian Legation, Manoel Coehlo Rodrigues, and his children, Regina and Maria, in Washington, DC. (Courtesy of the Library of Congress.)

This January 16, 1920, picture shows the commercial attaché of the Cuban Legation, P.A. Bonet; his wife, Madame Bonet; and their children, Evora and Porfirio A. Bonet, at the legation in Washington, DC. (Courtesy of the Library of Congress.)

This picture shows the children of the counselor of the Chilean Embassy, Sena Don Gustavo Munigaza Varela. The children are Eliza, 14; Mary, 8; Leopold, 11; and Gilberto, 2 months. (Courtesy of the Library of Congress.)

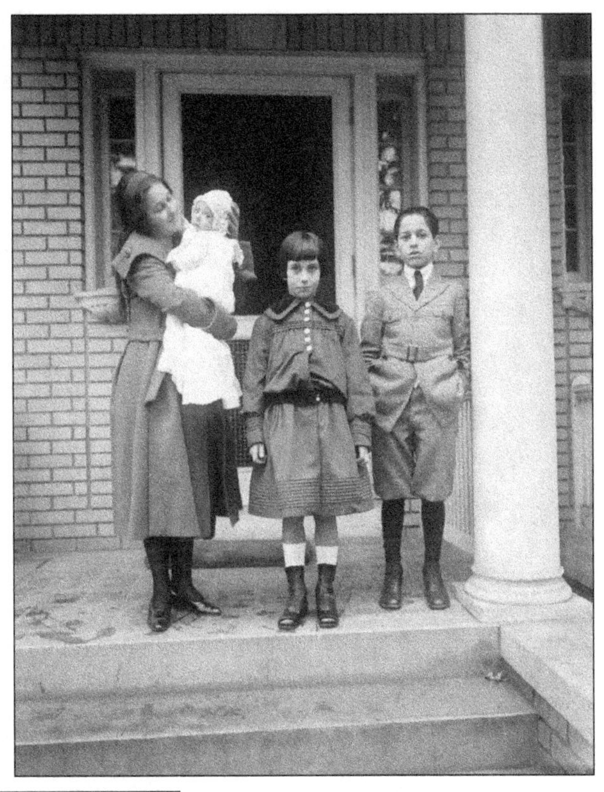

This photograph shows the minister from Paraguay to the United States, Eusebio Ayala, his wife, Marcelle Durand, and their son, Roger, upon their arrival in Washington, DC, on January 21, 1925, at the Wardman Park Hotel. Eusebio was the former president of Paraguay. (Courtesy of the Library of Congress.)

This picture shows Emilia and José Tellez, the children of Mexican ambassador Don Manuel Tellez, in the Mexican Room at the Mexican Embassy in Washington, DC, around 1925. (Courtesy of the Library of Congress.)

This image shows the Christmas party at the Mexican Embassy on December 26, 1925. The children are participating in the tradition of the piñata, a highlight of many Latin American parties. (Courtesy of the Library of Congress.)

In 1927, Mrs. Frank Barrows Freyer presented a talk on Peruvian women at the Woman's Universal Alliance Conference in Washington. The five models represent women over the years, including Mrs. Freyer (Maria Engracia Critcher) dressed in Spanish costume; Engracia Freyer in 17th-century dress; Betty Bratton in 18th-century dress; Mrs. Leslie Bratton (Emeline Wolfe Bratton) in the dress of a noblewoman of the vice-regal period; and Fidelia Gallardo, dressed as a Peruvian peasant. (Courtesy of the Library of Congress.)

This December 20, 1939, picture shows the children of diplomats in Washington, DC, participating in the Eighth Annual International Broadcast of "Merry Christmas" for the children of all nations. This broadcast was sponsored by the Washington Board of Trade's Greater National Capital Committee in cooperation with the National Broadcasting Company. The children are dressed in the costumes of their home countries and include many from Latin America. (Courtesy of the Library of Congress.)

On April 15, 1940, President Roosevelt addressed the board of the Pan American Union, later called the Organization of American States (OAS). The president called for unity among the republics of the Americas in maintaining peace. Secretary of State Cordell Hull attends the event with Dr. L.S. Rose, the director general of the Pan American Union, and ambassadors, ministers, and diplomats, including Peruvian Dr. Manuel de Freyre y Santander, Mexican Dr. Francisco Najera, Brazilian Dr. Carlo Martins, Chilean Dr. Alberto Cabero, Panamanian Dr. Jorge E. Boyd, Dominican Dr. Andre Pastorica, Bolivian Dr. Luis Fernando Gauchalla, Nicaraguan Dr. Deon De Byale, Paraguayan Dr. Horacio Fernandez, Guatemalan Dr. Enrique Lopez Herra, Cuban Dr. Jose T. Baron, Honduran Dr. Julian R. Caceres, Haitian Dr. Elie Lescot, Costa Rican Dr. Ricardo Beech, Uruguayan Dr. Jose Richling, Colombian Dr. Gabriel Turbay, Venezuelan Dr. Diogenes Escalante, Ecuadoran Capt. Colon Eloy Alfaro, and Salvadoran Dr. Hector David Castro. (Courtesy of the Library of Congress.)

Two

Emerging Community

As a national capital, Washington, DC, has drawn residents from throughout the world. Though small in number, these residents made and continue to make the metro area extremely diverse. The earlier Hispanic residents were comprised of diplomats and professionals working at the embassies and other institutions. There were also staff and domestic workers who came along with them. While some of these people moved on to new posts, others stayed and raised their children as first-generation Latinos.

Other institutions established early on include the Organization of American States (OAS) and the Pan American Health Organization (PAHO). The OAS began in 1889 with the first International Conference of America States. At this time, 18 American countries met to address political and economic issues. Later these countries formed the Pan American Union. PAHO was founded in Washington, DC, in 1902, to improve health and quality of life in the Americas.

As Europe was being rebuilt after World War II, the World Bank was established. The first executive director of the World Bank was Emilio Gabriel Collado, who was of Puerto Rican descent. Then, in 1959, the Inter-American Development Bank (IDB) was founded. The roots of the IDB are in the first meeting of Pan American Conference in 1890.

In the late 1950s and early 1960s, many Cuban and Dominican immigrants arrived because of revolution and political conflict in their countries. In the 1960s and 1970s, many South Americans arrived after facing severe political and economic difficulties. The many universities throughout the metro area also brought Hispanic scholars, their families, and many students from Latin America.

In the early 1950s, various business and community places began to serve the Hispanic residents of the DC metro area. In 1977, *El Pregonero*, the oldest Spanish-language newspaper in Washington, DC, was founded through the Catholic Archdiocese of Washington. *El Pregonero*'s missions has been to "offer a means of communication to the growing Hispanic population, informing the community in its own language, and providing guidance in its efforts to adjust to a new society."

Javier Malagón Barceló (1911–1991) was a refugee of the Spanish Civil War who after years of exile in the Dominican Republic and Mexico came to DC with his family to work at the OAS. A noted historian, he eventually became the cultural attaché of the Spanish Embassy focusing on building bonds between Spain and the Americas. A prideful Spaniard, he also embraced his American life and even became an avid Redskins fan. (Courtesy of Maria Helena Malagón.)

Helena Perenya Malagón (1913–2008) began working at PAHO in the late 1950s. She arrived in DC in 1953 with her family and an unusable degree in law. At PAHO, she translated health documents into Spanish from French, Italian, English, and Portuguese. She was also an accomplished pianist and seamstress. She and her husband, Javier, stayed in the DC area because her only daughter and grandchildren lived here. (Courtesy of Maria Helena Malagón.)

Family and friends of Javier and Helena Malagón, shown dancing, celebrate New Year's Eve in Washington, DC, in 1957. The Malagón family arrived in DC in 1953 with a plan to return to Spain but eventually settled in the area with their growing family and community of friends who had also immigrated from Spain, the Caribbean, and Latin America. Among the guests are Rafael Supervia, a professor at George Washington University, and his wife, Guillermina, who taught Spanish at Sidwell Friends. Like Javier and Helena Malagón, this couple fled Spain after the civil war. In 1939, both couples traveled from France to the Dominican Republic on the same ship, the *Lafayette*. (Both, courtesy of Maria Helena Malagón.)

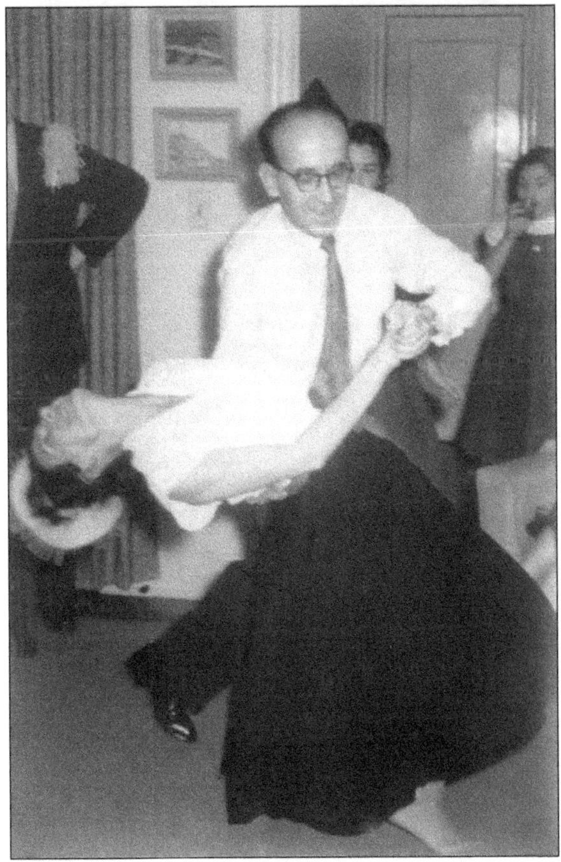

Pau Casals, Catalan cellist and conductor, is seated with Helena Malagón in her home in Bethesda, Maryland, in 1969. Helena and Javier Malagón, like their dear friend Pau Casals, were exiled from Spain after the Spanish Civil War. Whenever he came to Washington, he visited his friends in their home. (Courtesy of Maria Helena Malagón.)

Maria Helena and Helena Perenya Malagón are shown here in 1953 in Annapolis, Maryland. Today, Annapolis remains a nearby escape for Washingtonians seeking bay breezes and Chesapeake Bay blue crabs. Over the years, the Malagón family was just as likely to have an outdoor feast of crabs as paella. (Courtesy of Maria Helena Malagón.)

Maria Helena Malagón joins the annual safety patrol parade on the National Mall in 1954. She was a student at John Quincy Adams School. At this time, there were no programs for teaching English as another language. Having arrived in the area only the year before, this image shows how quickly children acculturate to their new surroundings. (Courtesy of Maria Helena Malagón.)

The Oyster School's sixth-graders pose for a class picture in 1956. Maria Helena Malagón, seated in the first row on the far left, was the only Spanish speaker in the class. Today, this school is the Oyster-Adams Bilingual School. It is a dual-language (English-Spanish) immersion school for pre-K to eighth-graders. (Courtesy of Maria Helena Malagón.)

The 1962 Sidwell Friends Cheerleaders included, from left to right, (bottom row) Nancy Adams, Judith Szathmari, Sandy Schinnerer, and Ripple Gilbert; (middle row) Margo Lee, Ellen Gay, and Mary Beale; (top row) Maria Helena Malagón. Maria Helena was the captain of the cheerleaders and the only Hispanic student in the class. She became Montgomery County Public School's ESOL director, leading language and support programs that were essential for the 1980s influx of immigrants. (Courtesy of Maria Helena Malagón.)

Upon his arrival in DC in 1956, Luis Federico Navarro (1939–1995) stands in Meridian Hill Park with his mother, Claudia Florentini Rios (right), and a family friend, Asuncion ? (left), from Spain. Claudia arrived in 1945 from Lima, Peru, to work as a domestic for a Peruvian diplomatic family. Claudia and Asuncion became close friends who met through their mutual friends from Spain, Vicente and Mimi Gonzalez. (Courtesy of Sheila Navarro.)

In 1963, Sheila K. Rose Navarro relaxes with Luis Federico Navarro at Meridian Hill Park. Luis grew up in the mountains of Huayopampa in the province of Canta, Peru. Sheila grew up in Logansport, Indiana. The couple met while working at the Science Information Exchange on Florida and Connecticut Avenues, Northwest. They married in 1962 at the Calvary Baptist Church on Eighth and H Streets Northwest. (Courtesy of Sheila Navarro.)

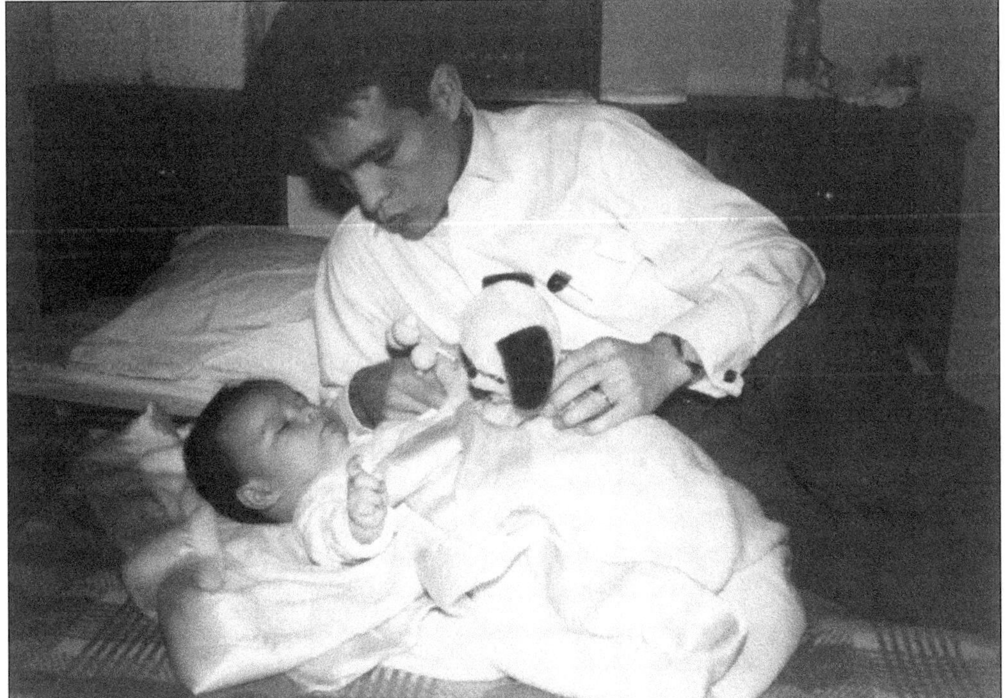

At their Columbia Road apartment, Luis F. Navarro plays with his son, Luis Antonio Navarro, born in 1963 at George Washington University Hospital. Luis F. Navarro, originally from Peru, became a certified public accountant in the District and later the director of cost and audit management at Health Services and Resources Administration (HRSA) in Rockville, Maryland, where he worked for 20 years. (Courtesy of Sheila Navarro.)

Luis F. Navarro and his son, Luis Antonio Navarro, enjoy Great Falls, Maryland, in the 1960s. Luis Antonio has grown up to become very involved in local and international politics. His permanent residence is in Silver Spring, Maryland, but he currently resides in the Republic of Georgia in Eurasia, where he serves as director of the National Democratic Institute. (Courtesy of Sheila Navarro.)

In the summer of 1965, Luis F. Navarro plays with his son, Luis Antonio, at the Iwo Jima Memorial in Virginia. After working in a sandwich shop in Virginia, Luis joined the US Army and was stationed in Germany from 1957 to 1961. He was classified as Caucasian in the Army. He is buried in Arlington National Cemetery. (Courtesy of Sheila Navarro.)

In 1970, Luis F. Navarro rides a train with his two-year-old daughter Lara Renee Navarro Roach, who was born at Sibley Hospital in Washington, DC. The train was part of an amusement park at the Takoma Park shopping center in Maryland. The Navarro family won tickets to the park after Luis Antonio had entered his name in a radio contest and won the title of King for the Day. (Courtesy of Sheila Navarro.)

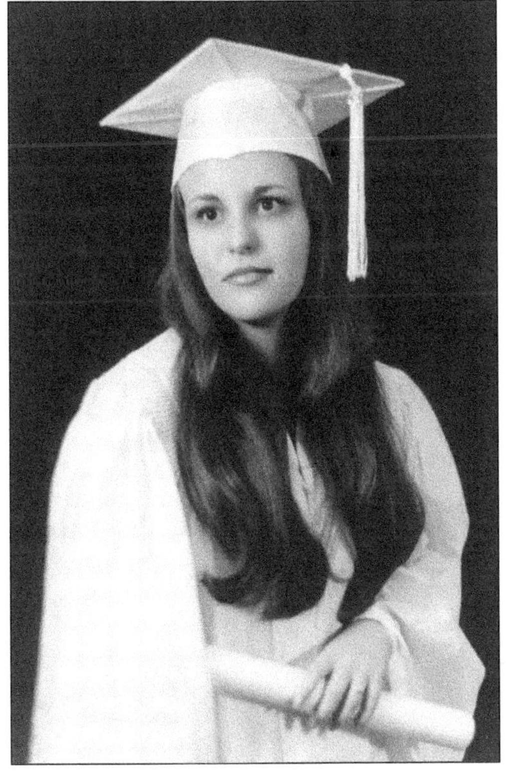

Ingrid Corratgé graduated from Blair High School in 1975. She and her mother, Yolanda Hidalgo, came to Maryland in 1972 from Madrid, Spain, where they lived after fleeing Cuba in 1970. Today, she works in the Division of ESOL/Bilingual Programs in Montgomery County Public Schools. She lives within a mile of her mother, three children, and three grandchildren in Gaithersburg, Maryland. (Courtesy of Ingrid Corratgé.)

Emma "Emy" Violand-Sanchez, who immigrated to the United States from Bolivia as a teenager, graduated from Mount Vernon High School in 1962. On the back of her high school graduation picture, she wrote, "Papito: Ya termino de subir la primera grada de mi vida, el bachillerato, espero y ruego a Dios seguir siempre adelante, y pagar el sacrificio que hacen por nosotros. Con todo amor Emi." Which translates to "Daddy: I have just finished the first stage of my life, receiving my high school diploma, I hope and pray to God that I keep moving forward, and repay the sacrifice that you have made for us. With all my love Emi" (Both, courtesy of Emma Violand-Sánchez.)

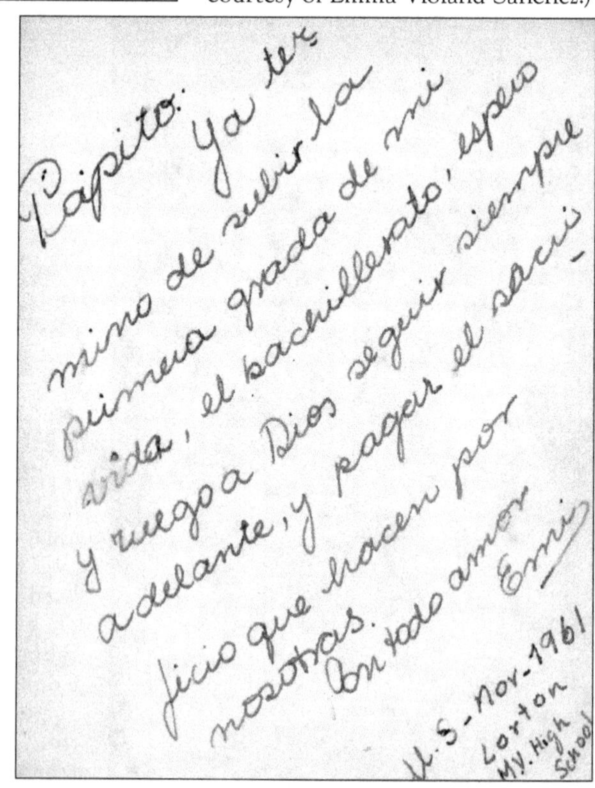

Papito: Ya ter-
mino de subir la
primera grada de mi
vida, el bachillerato, espero
y ruego a Dios seguir siempre
adelante, y pagar el sacri-
ficio que hacen por
nosotros.
Con todo amor
Emi

U.S.-Nov-1961
Lorton
MV. High
School

Emma Violand-Sánchez poses for a photograph along the Potomac River in 1963. She was born in Cochabamba, Bolivia, and at 16 she immigrated to the United States when her father was exiled from their home country. By 1976, Emma Violand-Sánchez was pursuing her passion—education—and she became the first Latina bilingual teacher in Arlington County. Today, she sits on the Arlington County School Board, the first Latina to do so. (Courtesy of Emma Violand-Sánchez.)

Juana Gonzalez immigrated to the United States from Canton La Estancia, Cacaopera, El Salvador, in 1978. There were few opportunities for her in El Salvador. This is the earliest picture of her in Maryland. Her first job in the United States was working as a housekeeper for a diplomatic family. Her childhood dream was to become a businesswoman. Today, she is the successful owner of a restaurant and food truck business. (Courtesy of Juana Gonzalez.)

The Gatti family emigrated from Asuncion, Paraguay, to the United States in 1968. From left to right at left are Miguel, Livia, Maria, Gustavo, and Rosanna Gatti enjoying the snow at their home in Bethesda, Maryland, soon after their arrival. Above, Gustavo and Livia Gatti pose for a snapshot before attending an event. The family moved to the DC area after Gustavo Gatti was offered a job as a junior lawyer at the Inter-American Development Bank (IDB). The family had planned to return to Paraguay after a few years, but the political situation in Paraguay worsened, and they made Maryland their home. Livia Gatti became a Spanish teacher and worked at Holton Arms School in Potomac, Maryland. She also became a docent at the Phillips Collection in Washington, DC. Today, their family includes three bilingual grandchildren who live in Washington, DC. (Both, courtesy of Livia Gatti.)

Three

Conflict in Central America

The nation's capital is unique in that it provides a stage where international and national issues often intersect with local people and community life. The long avenues and open spaces like the National Mall have long been used by people who gather to bring attention to issues, protest actions (or lack thereof), or to celebrate meaningful events. Some of the more public demonstrations in Washington, DC, regarding the conflicts in Central America during the 1980s and 1990s were protests against the wars in that region and rallies for greater awareness of human rights violations.

Poverty and inequality in Central America, particularly in El Salvador, Nicaragua, and Guatemala, reached severe levels in the 1970s. While elite families and transnational corporations gained more and more wealth from resources such as cotton, coffee, and cattle, the working class in these countries became poorer and more marginalized. The result was civil strife, rebellion, and then complicated wars that involved diverse groups of people and governments across the globe and lasted from the late 1970s to the early 1990s.

As the conflicts raged in Central America and refugees began arriving in large numbers in the Washington metropolitan area, organizations formed, and local residents, national personalities, and many people took to the streets to bring attention to the plight of the people of El Salvador, Guatemala, and Nicaragua. While many organizations drew attention to these issues, this chapter can only highlight some of them, such as the Sanctuary Movement, a religious and political organization, and the Committee in Solidarity with the People of El Salvador (CISPES), both founded in 1980.

In this photograph, many people participate in a mass as part of the Sanctuary Movement in Washington, DC, on September 26, 1986. The Sanctuary Movement formed to provide safe havens for refugees. More than 500 congregations participated in the movement. (Photograph by Rick Reinhard.)

Supporters of the Sanctuary Movement demonstrate in the streets of Washington, DC, on September 28, 1986. Christian, Jewish, Quaker, and other faith groups joined the movement as a way to provide refuge and assistance to the hundreds of thousands of individuals who entered the United States as they fled civil war and violence in their home countries. US immigration policies at the time made it nearly impossible for Central American exiles to be granted political asylum status. (Photograph by Rick Reinhard.)

Various demonstrations against United States' aid to the Contra movement in Nicaragua were held in Washington, DC. Above, demonstrators hold signs up in front of the Washington Marriott Hotel on April 15, 1985. At right, the Worby family—Laura, Carlos, and nine-month-old Celia—participate in an anti–Contra aid demonstration on the east steps of the Capitol Building on July 26, 1988. (Both photographs by Rick Reinhard.)

Maria Teresa Tula, founding member of the COMADRES (Committee of the Mothers Monsignor Romero) of El Salvador, addresses human rights demonstrators in DC on April 25, 1987. The COMADRES were modeled after the Mothers of the Plaza de Mayo, a group formed in the 1970s in Argentina that opposed the kidnapping and murder of political dissidents. During the war in El Salvador, thousands of innocent citizens, including Maria Teresa, were detained and tortured by the military. (Photograph by Rick Reinhard.)

Adolfo Perez Esquivel, Argentinean human rights activist and recipient of the 1980 Nobel Peace Prize, speaks at a Washington, DC, church in 1982. The portrait on the podium is that of Archbishop Oscar Romero, who was assassinated by government forces in El Salvador for speaking out against human rights abuses committed by the military. (Photograph by Rick Reinhard.)

Well-known Americans such as peace activist William Sloan Coffin (left), commentator Jim Wallis, and actors Ed Asner (center) and Raul Julia (far right), join protestors as they march from the Ellipse to the White House on March 24, 1990. An effigy of the Archbishop Oscar Romero, who was assassinated by Salvadoran military forces in 1980, is carried along the streets of DC. (Photograph by Rick Reinhard.)

People rally in front of the nation's capitol building to protest US involvement in El Salvador. The protestors hold coffins and crosses as symbols of the many who had already perished in the war. On the back right of the image there is a large sign with an image of the Archbishop Romero. (Photograph by Rick Reinhard.)

Police arrested 51 protestors at a Steps to Freedom rally that was led by the Committee in Solidarity with the People of El Salvador (CISPES) at the US Capitol grounds on October 16, 1989. CISPES was established in 1980 in Washington, DC, and Los Angeles to fight against US interventionist policies in El Salvador and to advocate for peace. (Photograph by Rick Reinhard.)

CISPES organized walkathons in the streets of Washington DC. At right, demonstrators carry signs in a walk held in 1989. Below, another group continues with the cause later in the year. (Both photographs by Rick Reinhard.)

A Salvadoran couple from Ahuachapán wave from their window in Washington, DC. Passing by their window is a 50-car caravan of supporters of the Farabundo Marti National Liberation Front (FMLN). The supporters are celebrating the Chapultepec Peace Accords, which were signed in January 1992 and ended 12 years of civil war in El Salvador. (Photograph by Rick Reinhard.)

Four

Community Organizations

Historically, community development and support organizations have been instrumental in facilitating the integration of immigrants into their new society. These groups develop and provide the services necessary to help new immigrants confront the challenges they face in their adopted country. Immigrant Latinos are no exception. They too have relied on such groups for assistance in job seeking, language instruction, immigration problems, political empowerment, and cultural and recreational activities. These community groups have also routinely facilitated communication and advocated with employers, government agencies, and institutions such as schools, hospitals, clinics, and courts. Although agencies serving Latinos in the Washington, DC, metro area have focused their attention primarily on education, including ESL classes, literacy classes, and computer training, they also have addressed the broad economic, social, and educational issues of special concern to Latinos and have placed special emphasis on youth services, such as sports activities, mentoring, child care, and gang-prevention initiatives. The advent of these groups dates back to the late 1960s, when the first large wave of Latino immigrants, the Cuban refugees, arrived in the Washington, DC, metropolitan area.

The economic, social, and emotional connections binding immigrants to their places of origin have stimulated the proliferation of a set of organizations known as hometown associations (HTA). These serve as clearinghouses for information on jobs, housing, and educational opportunities. They also act as sponsors of leisure activities particularly relevant to the group they serve and offer assistance with health issues and disaster relief. Almost every immigrant donor region in Latin America has its counterpart in the Washington, DC, metro area. Salvadorans alone, who represent more than 34 percent of the more than 700,000 Latinos residing in the Washington area, have over 14 hometown associations.

CARECEN directors Joaquin Dominguez Parada and Patricia Perillies established this center in 1981 to provide assistance to the then-growing Salvadoran community. Now known as the Latino Resource and Justice Center, CARECEN provides an array of social services to low-to-moderate-income Latinos living in DC and the adjacent areas in Maryland and Virginia. (Photograph by Rick Reinhard.)

The staff of CARECEN, previously known as the Central American Refugee Center, poses in front of its headquarters in Columbia Heights in 1986. (Photograph by Rick Reinhard.)

A CARECEN staff member meets with a community member to discuss her needs. In the 1980s, CARECEN contributed to the founding of both La Clinica del Pueblo and CASA de Maryland. (Photograph by Rick Reinhard.)

In 1991, a CARECEN worker assists a Salvadoran man in completing the required immigration application for Temporary Protection Status (TPS). Although US immigration policies in place in the 1980s made it nearly impossible for the majority of Salvadorans fleeing civil war to apply for refugee status, the Immigration Act of 1990 established the Temporary Protection Status program, which allowed eligible Salvadorans already in the United States to remain in the country legally on a temporary basis. (Photograph by Rick Reinhard.)

Dr. Juan Romagoza, director of La Clinica del Pueblo, leads a health class in 1989. La Clinica del Pueblo was established in 1983 as a community health clinic in Columbia Heights. Initially under the auspices of CARECEN, it became incorporated as a separate nonprofit organization in 1995. Since its inception, the clinic has provided free bilingual medical services to the poor, the uninsured, and primarily immigrant patients. (Photograph by Rick Reinhard.)

Juan Romagoza speaks at a community meeting in 1997. A medical doctor who fled El Salvador after being held in detention and tortured by Salvadoran government forces, Dr. Romagoza devoted 21 years to serving DC's Latino community through his exemplary work as director of the clinic from 1987 until 2008, when he retired and returned to his native El Salvador to establish HIV education programs and medical clinics for the underserved. (Photograph by Rick Reinhard.)

This 1996 photograph shows a Clinica del Pueblo patient being examined. Using a culturally appropriate approach, the Clinica del Pueblo serves the Latino and immigrant communities in the Washington, DC, area. The clinic was established in 1983 in response to the needs of the Central American refugees arriving in the DC area. (Photograph by Rick Reinhard.)

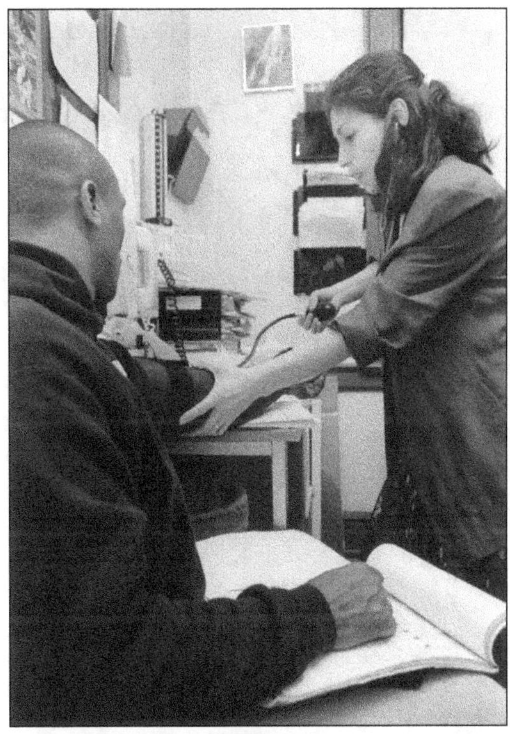

CASA de Maryland's first home was in the basement of the Takoma Park Presbyterian Church in Maryland. Sr. Mary Wendeln (back row) helps to distribute Christmas presents to Latino families in 1995. The Central American Solidarity Association (CASA) was established by local church congregations involved in the Sanctuary Movement in order to provide assistance to the thousands of Central Americans arriving in the area in the 1980s. (Courtesy of CASA de Maryland.)

Day laborers wait for prospective employers outside of a paint store in Silver Spring in 1992. CASA staff became concerned about the welfare of workers contracted as casual laborers as they often faced unfair treatment at the hands of private contractors. That, in addition to the growing resistance of business owners to the presence of workers congregating outside their storefronts, led CASA to establish a temporary day labor center. (Photograph by Rick Reinhard.)

This photograph from April 1992 shows a Montgomery County police officer speaking with a day laborer. He is asking her to help him get workers to move from the street corner to the new CASA de Maryland day laborer trailer set up as an office to help connect workers with prospective employers. (Photograph by Rick Reinhard.)

Workers stand outside the new temporary day laborer center that is housed in a trailer. The woman in the background is Betty Valdes, who in 1992 was the Montgomery County government's Latino Affairs representative. (Photograph by Rick Reinhard.)

In 1992, workers converse in the trailer that served as a CASA center in the earlier years. They are waiting to be contracted for day jobs, mostly including construction, landscaping, house painting, and remodeling. (Photograph by Rick Reinhard.)

Director of CASA de Maryland Gustavo Torres speaks at the inauguration of CASA's new headquarters in Langley Park on June 19, 2010. Since its inception in 1985, CASA has grown into the largest and most influential immigrant services organization, serving over 20,000 people and with multiple centers across the state of Maryland. Torres, a former journalist from Colombia who has served as director of CASA since 1993, has not only become one of the region's most influential Latino community leaders, but his advocacy work on behalf of immigrant rights issues has also gained him recognition at the national level. Pres. Barack Obama invited him to the White House alongside other top immigration advocates to discuss immigration reform in February 2013. *Washingtonian* magazine named him Washingtonian of the Year in 2002. (Courtesy of *El Tiempo Latino*.)

The Latin American Youth Center (LAYC) was founded in 1968 to address the needs of disenfranchised youth in an emerging Latino community. Over the decades, the LAYC has developed numerous successful programs and achieved a wide range of goals related to helping Latino youth and the community. In 2013, the LAYC received recognition by the S&I 100 as one of the "most impactful" nonprofit organizations nationwide. Above, a group poses in the late 1990s in front of the building that would become the new, and current, location of the LAYC on Columbia Road. Below, students meet at the LAYC, which provides a gathering place for them. (Both photographs by Rick Reinhard.)

Psychiatrist Dr. Ricardo Galbis, who was born in Cuba, speaks on the phone in his office at the organization he founded in 1970, Andromeda. This health care facility, which emphasizes the "importance of language, culture and a personal approach" to health care, is still serving a mostly Hispanic clientele in an underserved community in Washington, DC. From 1970 to 1971, Andromeda printed a Spanish-language newspaper, the first in DC. (Photograph by Sam Corum.)

Five

EDUCATION

The Washington, DC, metro area boasts some of the top-ranked public and private schools in the nation, many colleges and universities, and many technical and trade schools. Hispanic educators, including teachers, counselors, administrators, and staff, as well as university professors and those serving in elected positions, have contributed to the educational successes of generations of students, immigrants, and refugees at all levels of education.

Prior to the 1960s, the Hispanic students in the DC metro area were mostly the children of diplomats and embassy personnel or of employees of organizations such as the World Bank and the Organization of American States. However, after the 1959 Cuban revolution, many families fleeing Cuba came to the Washington, DC, area. By 1967, the large influx of Cuban refugees precipitated the need for English language instruction for school-age children. Counties in the area, such as Montgomery, Fairfax, and Arlington, became leaders in developing and instituting English language programs during this period. In the years to follow, and particularly in the 1980s during the height of the civil war in El Salvador, these programs were expanded to bring in more bilingual staff, including teachers, psychologists, parent specialists, counselors, educational assessment specialists, and clerical and support staff. Although students from El Salvador were by far the most numerous, every country in Latin America, as well as Spain, was represented by students in the English language programs. By 1992, eighteen percent of the staff in the English for Speakers of Other Languages (ESOL) program in Montgomery County was bilingual in Spanish and English. This was considered a necessity given that 45.1 percent of the students in that program were native Spanish speakers. Schools in the District of Columbia also responded to the demographic shift. In 1970, the Carlos Rosario International Public Charter School was founded by Sonia Gutierrez, and the Multicultural Career Intern Program (now known as Bell Multicultural High School) was established in 1980. Arlington County responded by developing the ESOL/High Intensity Language Training program. Educational leaders from ESOL programs in the metropolitan area met periodically as an informal group to share ideas on best practices for meeting the needs of their students.

On Hispanic Heritage Day in the mid-1990s, educators and other supporters of education gathered for this picture in front of the Montgomery County School Board in Rockville, Maryland. From left to right are Elizabeth Montgomery, Perche Rivas, Maria Helena Malagón, Teresa Wright, Vilma Montiel, Nivea Berrios, Jack Schoendorfer, Leonor Guillen, Cristina Riva-Chevez, George Dubreuil, Ana Stein, Aide Puertas, Henry Cisneros, Daniel Garcia, Grace Rivera-Oven, and unidentified. (Courtesy of Maria Helena Malagón.)

Jessica Martinez is surrounded by her fourth-grade classmates at Maryvale Elementary School in Rockville, Maryland. Jessica was born in Paraguay and immigrated to the United States when she was 10 years old. Today, she is a Montgomery College student. (Courtesy of Jessica Martinez.)

Juana Gonzalez stands with her son, Pablo Rubio. Pablo was born in El Salvador and immigrated to the United States to be with his mother, who came first to work as a domestic in the household of a diplomatic family. Her main motivation for coming to the United States was to educate her children. Today, Pablo holds a master's degree in social work and works with the community in Maryland. (Courtesy of Juana Gonzalez.)

Lo Nuestro, "Our Thing" in Spanish, performs for Hispanic Heritage Day in a Montgomery County public school. This dance troupe and a parent teacher association for Latinos were started by Einstein High School ESOL teacher Yolanda Glower, who immigrated to the United States from El Salvador in 1961. She came to the United States to provide better medical care for her son. When she first arrived in Maryland, Glower did not speak English. She went on to graduate from DC Teacher's College and receive a master's in special education from George Washington University. She also taught in an intensive English language center that supports immigrant students whose schooling had been interrupted in their homelands, volunteered at CASA de Maryland, and won the ESOL teacher of the year award in the 1990s. (Both, courtesy of Maria Helena Malagón.)

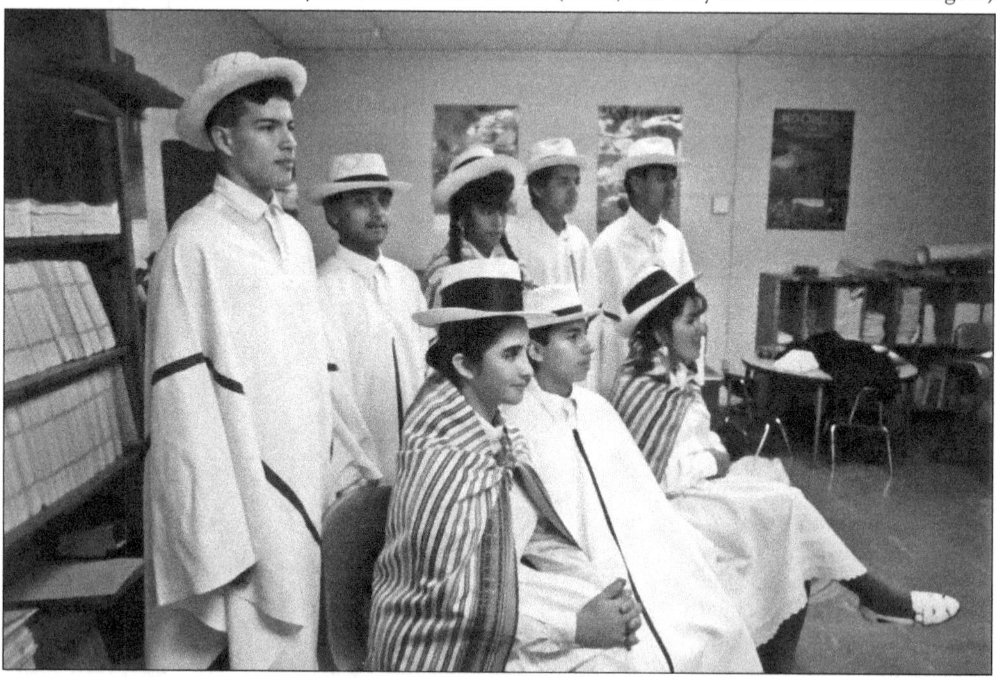

In 1989, Hispanic parents meet at a public school in Montgomery County, where devoted teachers such as Teresa Wright reach out to the parents to help the students. Programs for involving parents in the education of their children have been in place in the county for decades. (Both, courtesy of Linda Robinson.)

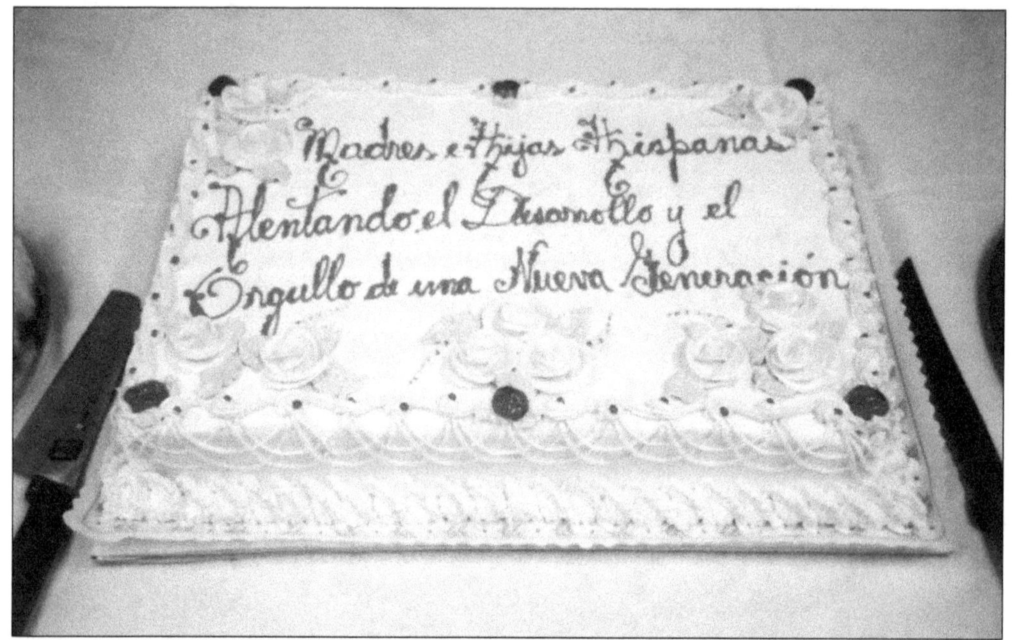

Montgomery County Public Schools became one of the first in the metro area to offer programs under the heading English for Speakers of Other Languages. The county also developed other programs to support the large immigrant community, such as the Mother-Daughter Conference, which was celebrated with this cake in April 1995 at Parkland Middle School in Montgomery County. A translation of the cake from Spanish to English reads, "Hispanic Mothers and Daughters Encouraging the Growth and Pride a New Generation." (Courtesy of Ana Jo Downs.)

The Educational Organization for United Latin Americans (EOFULA) has been serving Latino seniors in Washington for almost 40 years. EOFULA provides medical care, wellness services, group meals, and social services to seniors. (Courtesy of Olivia Cadaval.)

A General Educational Development (GED) class for Hispanic students is held at the Centro Comunal Unidad on February 12, 1991. This was a program sponsored by the Latin American Youth Center. (Photograph by Rick Reinhard.)

In this 1988 photograph, members of the Multicultural Career Intern Program (MCIP) in Columbia Heights pose after winning a tournament. The MCIP was founded in 1979 by Maria Tukeva to provide education for students with limited proficiency in English and low-income students. (Courtesy of Olivia Cadaval.)

A student receives guidance on applying to colleges at the Spanish Education Development Center (SED) in Washington, DC. The SED was founded in 1971, at first to provide day care for working Hispanic parents. This eventually became the first bilingual preschool in DC. Today, it offers many more programs for immigrant families. (Photograph by Rick Reinhard.)

Hispanic students at Montgomery College listen to a speaker at the Hispanic Academic Awards ceremony in April 2007. Montgomery College had a special academic achievement awards program recognizing the accomplishments of Latino students enrolled at the institution. (Courtesy of *El Pregonero*.)

A Montgomery College Hispanic student receives an Academic Achievement Award in April 2007. A significant number of the nation's Latino students attend community college prior to entering four-year colleges and universities. (Courtesy of *El Pregonero.*)

In May 2007, Carolina Peña graduated from Montgomery College's Scholars Program, a honors program that received recognition from Excelencia in Education for its retention of Hispanic college students. (Courtesy of *El Pregonero.*)

Carlos Rosario, one of the first and most well known Latino community organizers in Washington, DC, in the 1970s and 1980s, started an English as a Second Language program which eventually became a charter school under the leadership of educator Sonia Guiterrez. Today, the school provides adult education programs such as GED classes, ESOL, and vocational training programs for the city's large immigrant population. Students participate in a training class for chefs at Carlos Rosario International Public Charter School. (Courtesy of *El Tiempo Latino*.)

Identity staff member talks to young women participants. Identity is an after-school program providing support to Latino youth in Montgomery County and Prince George's County schools. The goal of the program is to provide students with experiences that will strengthen their sense of self and create a supportive community of peers. (Courtesy of *El Tiempo Latino*.)

"Latina Hace Historia" (Latina Makes History) reads the article in a Spanish-language newspaper in Virginia. Dr. Emma Violand-Sánchez celebrates her victory with the Honorable Walter Tejada, Arlington County board member and fellow Latino, after winning the election for the Arlington County School Board in 2009. (Courtesy of Emma Violand-Sánchez)

Martin O'Malley signs into law the Maryland DREAM Act on May 10, 2011. Standing behind him are Ana Sol Gutierrez and Victor Ramirez, two Maryland state legislators who were instrumental in getting the act passed. The Maryland DREAM Act allowed youth who had come to the USA as children but without legal status to be considered for instate tuition benefits upon meeting certain criteria, such as completion of high school in the state of Maryland and filing Maryland state taxes. (Courtesy of *El Tiempo Latino*.)

On May 10, 2011, students who lobbied for the Maryland DREAM Act celebrate on the steps of the Maryland State Capitol their hard won victory for the Maryland DREAM Act. Some of the students are wearing CASA de Maryland T-shirts, as that organization was key along with other organizations in supporting the needs of the many undocumented youth living in Maryland. Although many of the youth have lived in Maryland since a young age, they often were not able to attend a state college because of the high cost of out-of-state tuition. (Courtesy of *El Tiempo Latino*.)

Six

Latino Politics

Latino leaders have increasingly participated in the political systems of DC, Maryland, and Virginia. This civil engagement is important for providing representation of the Hispanic interests across the area. The governments of DC, Maryland, and Virginia have established commissions focused on these issues as well. DC's mayor has had an Office of Latino Affairs (OLA) since 1976. The Maryland Commission on Hispanic Affairs has been addressing the community's economic, educational, health, political, and social affairs since the 1980s. The Virginia Latino Advisory Commission, created in 2003, became the Virginia Latino Advisory Board in 2005. Hispanic politicians throughout the metro area have been advocating for decades for improvements in education, immigration reform, health care, job access, and other social services. Notable among these pioneers are Ana Sol Gutierrez in Maryland and Walter Tejada in Virginia, who are both first-generation Americans from El Salvador. Also important in the politics of the area are the long-standing organizations such as CASA de Maryland, which has advocated for and supported the community since its founding in the basement of a church in Takoma Park in 1985, and the Spanish Speaking Community of Maryland, founded in 1967 in Takoma Park, Maryland.

The importance of including civic leaders from various cultural backgrounds in a diverse metropolitan area is underscored when tensions and conflicts increase within a community. In 1991, for example, the Mount Pleasant riots, or *disturbios* in Spanish, which lasted for four days, reflected more than just anger about a shooting incident. The disturbios were sparked by the incident but reflected the anger of a community that felt marginalized and underrepresented.

Today, the streets of Washington, DC, continue to provide a place for expressing political tensions and demanding reforms. The DREAM Act and immigration reform are two of the more recent issues that have been highlighted on this local, national, and international stage. Notable Hispanic political leaders include Tom Perez, the nation's 26th secretary of labor, whose family hails from the Dominican Republic. Perez's political career includes membership on the Montgomery County Council.

In response to a growing anti-immigrant sentiment across the country, the Latino National March (*La Marcha*) brought 25,000 demonstrators to Washington on October 12, 2006. It was the first national immigration rally to take place in Washington, DC, which called for pro-immigrant demonstrators from other across the country to converge on the Ellipse near the White House in order to advocate for a series of reforms aimed at helping the immigrant community. Many demonstrators held signs and placards showing their support for the United States and their desire to be recognized for their contributions to the country. Pictured at left, six-year-old Kevin, born in the United States to Salvadoran parents, holds a sign as his parents listen to the speeches at the Ellipse. Below, a Salvadoran father holds his child at a local immigration rally in 1994. (Both photographs by Rick Reinhard.)

On May, 6, 1991, residents speak to the press after a night of anti-police street protests following the shooting of 30-year-old Salvadoran Daniel Gomez by a DC metropolitan police officer in the predominately Latino neighborhood of Mount Pleasant. The incident set off street riots as young Latinos, many of whom had fled civil war in Central America, responded to years of perceived harassment and unfair treatment by local authorities. (Photograph by Rick Reinhard.)

On, May 7, 1991, two days after the shooting, riot police check the identification of a Latina woman on her way home from work. A dusk-to-dawn curfew was imposed in response to the civil unrest. (Photograph by Rick Reinhard.)

At left, the executive director of CARECEN, Pedro Aviles, leads a street march on the first anniversary of the Mount Pleasant riots in May 1992. Aviles, a Mount Pleasant resident, became involved in advocating for the rights of Latinos in DC following the Mount Pleasant riots. He was appointed by then DC mayor Sharon Pratt to the first DC Latino Civil Rights Task Force. In the picture below, dated 1996, the task force is awarding a certificate of recognition to Raul Yzaguirre from the National Council of La Raza, who was instrumental in negotiating with the DC government and police to bring about positive change for the Latino community. (Both photographs by Rick Reinhard.)

Bolivian-born Beatriz "BB" Otero (center), pictured in 1992, the first Latina to run for a seat on the DC Public School Board, campaigns in Ward 1—Mount Pleasant, Adams Morgan, and Shaw—which includes neighborhoods with the highest number of Latino students in DC. (Photograph by Rick Reinhard.)

BB Otero is pictured here with her family in 1992. A former teacher, BB Otero founded CentroNia, a key organization in the DC Latino community dedicated to serving the needs of children and families. She also was instrumental in establishing DC charter schools and is a longtime champion for social justice for DC's ethnic communities. In 2011, DC mayor Vincent Gray appointed Otero as deputy mayor of health and human services. (Photograph by Rick Reinhard.)

Cuban-born Emilio Perche-Rivas (second from right) was pivotal in establishing and directing the Spanish Speaking Community of Maryland in 1977, one of the first Maryland organizations to provide social services to the Latinos in Montgomery and Prince George's Counties. A staunch advocate for the Latino community, he was instrumental in garnering support from local and state officials in order to address the most pressing needs of the growing Latino population. (Courtesy of Linda Robinson.)

Members of the Maryland Governor's Commission on Hispanic Affairs attend the annual Gala Dinner-Dance in September 1990. Standing from left to right are Roberto Laureano, Fr. Dalton Downs, Willie Clark, Gov. Parris N. Glendening, and Constance Clark. Ana Jo Downs is seated (left) with the secretary of the commission and John and Ruby Hammond. (Courtesy of Fr. Dalton Downs.)

Janitors and parking lot attendants, members of Service Employees International Union (SEIU) Local 82, protest in the streets of DC on March 21, 1995. As part of the protest, demonstrators petitioned for higher wages and better working conditions. The Justice for Janitors movement started in 1987 and sought to unionize thousands of service workers in DC, many of whom were Latino immigrants. (Photograph by Rick Reinhard.)

Pixie Pete, the famous organizing mascot of SEIU, gets arrested at the Justice for Janitors march on March, 21, 1995, as demonstrators block the streets at Seventeenth Street and Pennsylvania Avenue, Northwest. A target of the demonstration was Carr Realty Corporation, a large real estate development company that hired many janitors and parking lot attendants across the city. Parking lot attendants and janitors brought allegations of poor treatment by Carr Realty. (Photograph by Rick Reinhard.)

On May 26, 1996, the DC Latino Civil Rights Task Force sponsored the Fourth Annual Latino Community Congress. The young woman on the left is being fingerprinted for her US citizenship application. The task force also sponsored voter registration drives in order to encourage eligible Latinos with US citizenship to participate in the electoral process. (Photograph by Rick Reinhard.)

Jaime Contreras, kneeling on the right at a 1989 party, immigrated with his family to the United States from El Salvador in 1988. It was at this time that he became involved in union activities. He attended Bell Multicultural High School during the day, and at night, he cleaned buildings. Today, Jaime Contreras is the vice president of the 32BJ's Capital Area District's Services Employees International Union (SEIU). (Courtesy of Jamie Contreras.)

Jaime Contreras addresses supporters at an immigration rally on the Washington Mall on April 10, 2006. Contreras, a civil war refugee from El Salvador, became a citizen in 1996. In addition to his position at the SEIU, Jaime Contreras founded and chaired the National Capitol Immigrant Coalition (NCIC), a group of organizations calling for immigration reform in the political heartland of America. The NCIC became instrumental in the mobilization and coordination of demonstrations involving millions of Latinos and other immigrants across the nation in 2006. Maryland governor Martin O'Malley acknowledged Jaime's contributions to immigrant rights in 2008 by appointing him as a member of the Council for New Americans, an initiative aimed at facilitating the integration of immigrants into the economic and social fabric of that state. Jaime lives in College Park with his wife and two of his four children. (Courtesy of *El Tiempo Latino.*)

Above, 15-year-old Elizabeth Reyes (center) and 18-year-old Fanny Roque (right), students at DC's Bell Multicultural High School, gather in Washington's Malcolm X Park in anticipation of the La Marcha, a march in support of immigrant rights. The October 12, 1996, march culminated at the Ellipse. Students such as these participated in immigration rallies across the country as a way to fight back against the growing anti-immigrant, anti-Latino sentiment and to support immigration reform that would benefit their families. A decade or more later, Latino youth would take a pivotal role in sparking the Dreamers movement, which seeks to grant legal status to individuals who were brought to the United States as children but are unable to fully participate in the civic life of the country they call home because they lack legal status. Below, marchers hold a sign, "Latino Power," at the Ellipse during 1996's La Marcha. (Both photographs by Rick Reinhard.)

Nancy Navarro was born in Caracas, Venezuela. She has lived in Montgomery County since the late 1990s. Currently, she is the president of the Montgomery County Council. She has served on the Montgomery County Board of Education and received numerous awards, including the Heart of the Community Award from the Community Teachers Institute and the Hispanic Chamber of Commerce of Montgomery County Leadership award. She and her family live in Montgomery County. (Photograph by Maria Sprehn-Malagón)

Maryland state senator Victor Ramirez speaks at a community event in 2006. Senator Ramirez moved to Maryland from El Salvador as a child. He served as a delegate from 2003 to 2011 and was instrumental in helping to draft the Maryland DREAM Act, which allows eligible students who were brought into the United States without legal status as children to be considered for instate college tuition benefits. (Courtesy of *El Pregonero*.)

Walter Tejada, shown here with Virginia governor Tim Kaine (left), has come far since the days of his youth when he polished shoes in a *supermercado* in El Salvador to help his family. He immigrated when he was 13 and studied government and communication at George Mason University. Today, he is the chairman of the Arlington County Board and an active member of various immigrants' rights and civil rights organizations. (Courtesy of *El Pregonero*.)

Ana Sol Gutiérrez, born in El Salvador and raised in Montgomery County, became the first Latina to serve on the Maryland General Assembly when she was elected in 2003. In her career, she has served on many boards and has been a strong supporter of education. She was on the Montgomery County Board of Education from 1990 to 1998, her first elected position. (Courtesy of *El Tiempo Latino*.)

Seven

Occupational Diversity

The metro area's Hispanic community overall is more educated and more affluent than those of other metropolitan areas. Hispanics here work in all sectors and levels of society and represent an extremely diverse workforce. Data from the US Census Bureau, though, indicate that Latinos are more likely to have jobs in the construction and service-related industries than other ethnic groups. These higher rates are due in part to the higher rate of people with limited English proficiency.

The increasing number of Latino residents in the area has resulted in the establishment of educational and social programs, as well as businesses catering to their specific preferences. Bilingual and multilingual Spanish-speaking teachers, social workers, doctors, and nurses are increasing in numbers. In business, the area has seen the establishment of Hispanic-owned currency exchanges, shipping services, grocery stores, and ethnic restaurants. In Montgomery County alone, the US Census Bureau registered the existence of 11,547 (10 percent of the total) Latino-owned firms in 2007.

This region continues to be home to Latinos of very high levels of educational attainment who are employed by international organizations, such as the World Bank, embassies, the Organization of American States, and the Inter-American Development Bank. Like their predecessors, some of them will eventually end up permanently settling in the area. The metro area is also home to a growing group of Latino professionals succeeding in their chosen professions. These Latinos are high achievers who are exerting influence in all work spheres. They are entrepreneurs, business leaders, lobbyists, doctors, educators, lawyers, strategists, politicians, and much more.

The grand marshal (or *gran mariscal*) of the 17th Annual Hispanic Festival, a 25-year-old construction worker from El Salvador, waves at the crowds on July 26, 1987. He was selected as grand marshal as a symbol of the important role undocumented workers played in the development of the Washington, DC, Latino community. Although the construction workers are mostly unseen, their labor becomes the places where DC residents work, eat, play, and rest. (Photograph by Rick Reinhard.)

On April 24, 1992, day laborers pass the time waiting for work by singing *rancheras*, a favorite musical style enjoyed by many Central Americans. Day laborers were hired for the variety of handyman skills they possessed, including carpentry, painting, and landscaping. (Photograph by Rick Reinhard.)

Isabelino Gaona attends to a client's first haircut in Camillo's Barbershop, a place that has been in business in Washington, DC, since 1965. Gaona immigrated to the United States from Paraguay in the 1970s. Today, he is part of a larger Paraguayan community that includes his brother and sister, who are also hairstylists. (Courtesy of Oilda Gaona.)

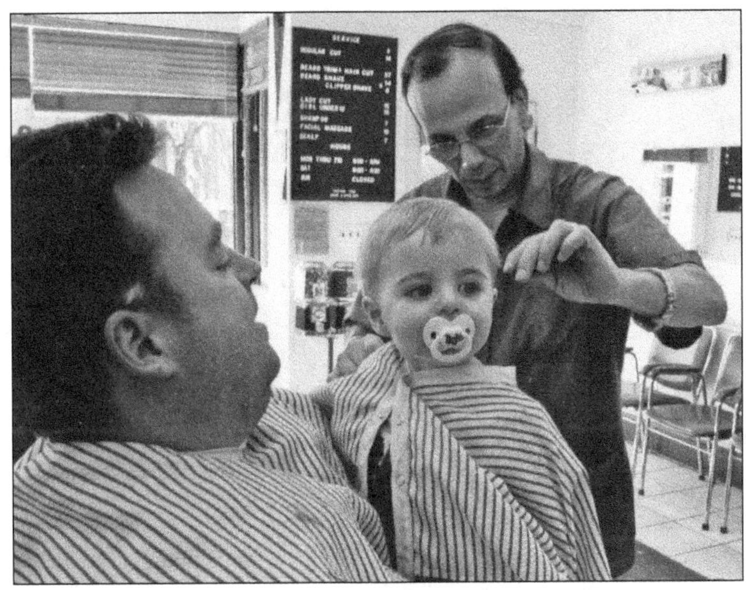

Owners of the Casa Veiga pose with a patron in front of their store on Flower Avenue in Silver Spring, Maryland. The Veigas opened one of the first Hispanic markets in Silver Spring. They are originally from Cuba. The date of the photograph is unknown, but it is likely from the 1980s. (Courtesy of *El Pregonero*.)

As a teenager, Neftali Granados of Guatajiagua, Morazán, El Salvador, saw little opportunity for his future, as the family farm was unable to support them. In the 1970s, he left and became a merchant marine. The country's civil war thwarted his plans in El Salvador and he immigrated to the DC area in 1982 with only the clothes on his back. With a chuckle he tells the story of purchasing the suit he is wearing, left, at K-Mart in Langley Park to attend a wedding. Five other men wore the same inexpensive suit to the wedding. Below, he stands with his daughter, Monica Delgado, in front of the Center Market Morazán in downtown Gaithersburg in 2013. Granados and his wife, Armida, have become successful entrepreneurs, owning three markets. They have raised three children and are now grandparents. (Both, courtesy of Neftali Granados.)

Virginia-based Todos Supermarket's owner, Carlos Castro, immigrated to the United States from El Salvador, where he lived with his nine siblings in a small house without running water or a sewer system. Today, he is the owner of a lucrative business with 140 employees. He recently became a member of the board of directors of Northern Virginia Community College. (Courtesy of Carlos Castro.)

On February 26, 2006, President Saca (center) of El Salvador receives the Person of the Year Award from the US Salvadorian Chamber of Commerce, based in Virginia. In 2007, President Saca returned to DC to sign a landmark agreement with key Salvadoran-American chambers of commerce, partnering Salvadoran and Salvadoran-American businesses. Salvadoran-Americans generated close to $3.3 billion in remittances, a significant financial contribution to El Salvador. (Courtesy of *El Pregonero*.)

This Eighteenth Street view shows two of the earlier Latino restaurants in Washington, DC: El Pollo Primo and El Tazumal. Neither of these restaurants is here today. While this neighborhood was a central place for many Latino immigrants in the latter 20th century, today many have moved to the suburbs, where Latino restaurants have become numerous. (Courtesy of Olivia Cadaval.)

Juana Gonzalez, owner of Juanita's Restaurant in Rockville, Maryland, poses in front of her car, two food trucks, and restaurant in Rockville, Maryland, in the 1980s. Gonzalez, originally from Cacaopera, El Salvador, came to the United States in 1978 because there were so few opportunities in her home country. Her first job in Maryland was working as a domestic for a diplomatic family. Her childhood dream had always been to become a businesswoman. (Courtesy of Juana Gonzalez.)

Jose Andres, internationally renowned chef, restaurateur, and owner of ThinkFoodGroup, is originally from Mieres, in Asturias, Spain, and settled in the Washington area in the 1990s. In addition to his businesses, Jose Andres works toward solving food and nutrition problems, both locally and globally. In the spring of 2013, at George Washington University, where he teaches, he made a paella to celebrate the end of the course. The paella was eight feet across. (Courtesy of Jose Andres.)

Patricia "Pati" Jinich, born and raised in Mexico City, serves up recipes and cuisine to the Washington, DC, area and internationally through her TV show, cookbooks, and blog. Her cooking career started in 2007 when she left her job as a political analyst and began the culinary program Mexican Table at the Mexican Cultural Institute. She lives in Chevy Chase, Maryland. (Photograph by Michael Ventura.)

Martin Mayorga pauses for a picture in front of bags of coffee imported from Nicaragua in the roasting facility in Rockville, Maryland. He was born in Guatemala and raised in Nicaragua. He and his wife, Kerry, founded Mayorga Coffee in 1997. Today, they have 100 employees. Recently, the Mayorgas established the Mayorga Latino Leadership Scholarship at Montgomery College with a major gift to the Montgomery College Foundation. Martin is an alumnus of Montgomery College. (Photograph by Maria Sprehn-Malagón.)

Benjamin Hernandez, whose father is a Mexican immigrant, is the founder and chief executive officer of NuMat Technologies, an award-winning technology company specializing in the design of high performance nanomaterials for the oil and gas, semiconductor, and health care industries. Ben, a Wootton High School graduate from Rockville, Maryland, earned a master's in business administration from the Kellogg School of Management, a juris doctorate from Northwestern University School of Law, and a bachelor's of science from the McCormick School of Engineering at Northwestern University. NuMat's team won the 2012 Rice Business Plan Competition (RBPC) "World Championship," taking home $874,000 in investments and cash grants and the honor of ringing the closing bell at Nasdaq in August of that year in a very contested field numbering 42 teams culled from 1,600 entries. His younger sister, Daniela Hernandez-Fujigaki (right), now a high school junior, was also the recipient of a grand prize, a $20,000 scholarship for her award-winning essay addressing the growing income disparity in the United States from the 2012 Junior Achievement Essay Competition organized by the Junior Achievement of Greater Washington. (Courtesy of Ben Hernandez.)

Alba Robinson-Contreras is seen here at her office at the Spanish Speaking Community (La Comunidad Hispana) on Riggs Road in Langley Park in 1992. She served as director of the Riggs Road office, where she provided social services to the Latino community and advocated for its needs with local governmental officials. (Courtesy of Linda Robinson.)

Alba Robinson Contreras visits an elderly resident in a senior residential apartment building where many Hispanic elderly lived. Through her position at the Spanish Speaking Community, she worked closely with Spanish-speaking senior citizens, helping them to obtain services such as Meals on Wheels, coordinating transportation to doctor visits, and organizing recreational activities. (Courtesy of Linda Robinson.)

Rev. Canon Dalton Downs (left), originally from Nicaragua and former rector of St. Timothy's in Washington, DC, poses with his wife, Ana Jo Downs (right), originally from Puerto Rico, and Vice Pres. Al Gore (center) during a White House event for the Organ and Donors Initiative, which focuses on educating and encouraging donations among minority populations. Father Downs's heart transplant, a "gift of life" from Dawn Alexander, a friend and parishioner of St. Timothy's, was highlighted at the event. (Courtesy of Fr. Dalton Downs.)

Alvaro Molina-Cruz was born in Guatemala and holds a doctorate in Biomolecular Chemistry from the University of Wisconsin-Madison. He is a scientist at the National Institute of Allergy and Infectious Diseases (NIAID), Laboratory of Malaria and Vector Research, National Institutes of Health, in Bethesda, Maryland. His research focuses on the factors that determine malaria transmission. He resides in Montgomery County with his wife, Marcia, and his children, Sophia and Fernando. (Courtesy of Jose Luis Ramirez.)

Spanish-speaking police officer Esteban Pacheco became the police liaison between the force and the Takoma Park Hispanic community in 1991. He worked to dispel the fear that many immigrants have of police and to provide the necessary communication between the community and the police force. (Courtesy of *El Pregonero.*)

Officer Rosa Roldan-Torres is a highly experienced officer of the Metropolitan Police Department (MPD), serving both the MPD's Latino Liaison Unit and Gay and Lesbian Liaison Unit (GLLU). As a *boricua* (Puerto Rican) and lesbian, she has a very specific skill set that she uses to assist the MPD with cases involving member of the Latino and LGBT communities. She is a familiar presence in Latino festivals, community gatherings, and schools. (Courtesy of the Latino LGBT History Project.)

Colombian-born Dr. Maria Cecilia Zea is a professor of psychology at the University of Maryland. She is also the director of the Latino Health Research Center (LHRC) at George Washington University. She became a research scientist because she "wanted to make a contribution to the knowledge base about Latinos in the United States . . . [based] on firsthand knowledge of many issues Latinos face in the U.S., and an insider understanding of Latino culture." (Courtesy of the Latino LGBT History Project.)

Catherine M. Pino is the cofounder and principal of D&P Creative Strategies, a company that she and partner Ingrid Duran founded in 2004 to increase the role of corporate, legislative, and philanthropic efforts in addressing the concerns of Latinos, women, and gay, lesbian, bisexual, and transgender (GLBT) communities. In 2004, she was named a Latina of Excellence by *Hispanic Magazine*. (Courtesy of the Latino LGBT History Project.)

Paola Andaló served as the editor in chief of *El Tiempo Latino*, the Spanish language newspaper affiliated with the *Washington Post*. *El Tiempo Latino* was founded in 1991 and bought by the *Washington Post* in 2004. Andaló worked as reporter and editor for the newspaper with the largest circulation in Argentina before immigrating to the United States. She and her family have made the Washington, DC, area home. (Courtesy of *El Tiempo Latino*.)

Affectionately known as the "Mars Czar," Orlando Figueroa, formerly the director of the NASA Mars Exploration Program, is pictured here with his wife, Josephine. The US government recruited Figueroa and other graduates from the prestigious University of Puerto Rico–Mayagüez Engineering School. This group of Puerto Rican engineers formed the "Exiled Engineers" alumni group that would gather for picnics with *plena* and *bomba* music at Blobs Park in Jessup in the 1990s. (Courtesy of Orlando Figueroa.)

Eight

Fiestas, Futbol, and the Arts

The expressive culture of the Latinos in the Washington, DC, metro area is infinitely broad and continuously generated. It reflects a shared sense of identity among Latinos in the DC area that is different from other cities. Individual and ethnic differences are obviously visible as well. Latino expressive culture is seen in fine art, street art, performance art, play, and leisure.

In the art of Latino DC, the Wilson Center complex figures prominently, as it housed the Latin American Youth Center, El Centro de Arte, and the Rumba School. Many dance clubs also contributed to the Latino art vibe. Night clubs like the former Chelsea's in Georgetown attracted the best salsa dancers in the area on Friday nights, and in Arlington, Virginia, well-known Latin dance bands would perform at Cecilia's, now known as the Salsa Room. Cuban-owned Habana Village in Adams Morgan was a favorite of many Latin dancers in the 1980s and 1990s, and after a fire and a brief closing it reopened. Perhaps the most visible and enduring expression of Latino cultural expression, however, is the Hispanic Festival, which began more than 40 years ago.

Hispanic fine arts have a long history in the DC area and continue today. The Mexican Cultural Institute's murals were painted by Mexican muralist Roberto Cueva del Rio in the 1930s. In addition, the Art Museum of the Americas, which the OAS established in 1976, houses important works of art collected by Cuban-born Jose Gomez Sicre, a DC resident, who was appointed the museum's chief of the visual arts in 1948. Among notable artists in DC is Septima Webre, the Cuban-American artistic director of the Washington Ballet, who was appointed in 1999. Septima Webre will often mention that "Cubans dance before they can walk."

Like festivals and religious rituals, sports can also express identity and reflect values. Perhaps no other sport can better reflect Latino culture than soccer (or *futbol*). This sport, which has European roots, particularly in England, spread throughout Latin America in the 19th century. By the mid-1800s, Chile, Argentina, and Uruguay had soccer clubs. In time, the sport was brought to its current popularity in the DC area, in part due to the waves of Latino immigrants who have been arriving for decades.

Thousands line the streets for the annual Latino Festival parade in Washington, DC, in the mid-1980s. The parade, dance, drama, music, and food form the base of the festival, which was centered at Columbia Road between Sixteenth Street and Kalorama Road in the Northwest area of Washington, DC. The festival started out as a half-day event in 1970 with 10,000 people. Five years later, it became a weeklong celebration of community and social ties. In 1987, an estimated 200,000 people attended the 17th Annual Latino Festival, which had more than 200 food kiosks and 40 music bands. In a July 27, 1987, *Washington Post* article, Norma Small-Warren, a Howard University chemistry professor and native of Panama, was quoted as saying that Latinos are "used to having big carnivals. In the United States and Washington, these don't exist. This is our one chance to release what we've suppressed all year." She also stated that the festival makes immigrants "feel like we've gone home for one afternoon." (Photograph by Rick Reinhard.)

The participants in the Hispanic Festival represented many countries. This one, from the Dominican Republic, moves down the street to the rhythms of a Dominican band in the 1978 Hispanic Festival. Many Dominicans immigrated to the DC area in the late 1950s and 1960s for both political and economic reasons. (Photograph by Michael Hoyt.)

In the earlier festivals, the parade floats were cars, vans, and trucks decorated in a theme that reflected the country of origin of the participants. This van has Maryland license plates and is decorated with Mexican flags and blankets typical of Mexico. (Courtesy of Olivia Cadaval.)

The Hispanic Festival was comprised of many different units including an individual, often with a flag, a *comparsa* (a carnival troupe with music and dance), a car, a float, a truck, and a truck with a flatbed. Above, the Costa Rican unit of the 1986 Hispanic Festival elaborately decorated a car for the parade. In 2009, the country of Costa Rica scored the highest in the Happy Planet Index. Below, a car from the Peruvian unit is decorated with flags, blankets, and llama effigies. The llama is the national symbol of Peru, reflecting both its spiritual and economic importance for this Andean country. (Both, courtesy of Olivia Cadaval.)

The Hispanic Festival parades included many units comprised of decorated cars and trucks as well as trucks hauling flatbeds. These units were often nationalistic, reflecting the presence of many of the Latin American countries in Washington, DC. As Smithsonian scholar Olivia Cadaval has pointed out, these parade units were more about pride in the local DC community than national allegiance. These units based on a country of origin were formed mostly through church networks or social clubs. Above, a float truck from Guatemala, pulling a flatbed, expresses the indigenous roots of Guatemalans, the Maya. (Courtesy of Olivia Cadaval.)

Individual people also formed part of the Hispanic Festival parade. Some would carry flags or comprise part of a comparsa (a carnival troupe with music and dance). Shown here is a participant from Panama. (Courtesy of Olivia Cadaval.)

During the 1987 Hispanic Festival, one of the many costumed participants in the Latino Festival parade dazzles the onlookers with her fantastic dress and dance. She is part of a comparsa. Often, these comparsas would form the end of the parade. (Photograph by Rick Reinhard.)

After recently arriving from Chicago, Mexican-born Olivia Cadaval reflected on her reaction when she attended the Hispanic Festival in the mid-1970s in Washington, DC: "The sense of solidarity among the mostly Latino crowds surprised and attracted me. I experienced an *ambiente* [cultural ambience] that was markedly different from that of the everyday American lifestyle to which I had become accustomed. The food, the dancing, the language, the expressive gestures and tones of voice evoked a memory of home and a longing for community for the first time since I had come to this country." Above, an unidentified woman waves to the crowd. At right, a participant expresses his Peruvian heritage. (Both photographs by Michael Hoyt.)

Representations of the myriad of cultures within the Latin American countries are visible in these photographs of the Hispanic Festival. Most years, there were about 20 different nations represented at the festival. In these July 1992 Hispanic Festival photographs, participants dance and play music as they perform in elaborate costume on the streets of Washington, DC. Below, the Bolivian unit performs the traditional folk dances such as the *saya* and the *caporales*, both based on indigenous Andean and Afro-Bolivian rhythms, instruments, and aesthetics. These dances reflect the merging of many cultural groups and time periods, including the Spanish Colonial period. (Both photographs by Michael Hoyt.)

Many of the Hispanic Festival participants carried flags that represented their countries of origin. In this photograph, about 10 different countries from Latin America are represented. (Courtesy of Olivia Cadaval.)

In this street scene shot during the Hispanic Festival parade are participants on foot and in cars. The float in the background is one from Colombia. The festival was a place both to represent Latino unity and to express cultural and national differences. (Courtesy of Olivia Cadaval.)

The Hispanic Festival *kioskos*, or outdoor "fast-food" stands, sold diverse foods from many different Latin American countries. Olivia Cadaval points out how the kioskos shared a marketplace arrangement, presentation, and delivery reflective of the Latin American system. Some of the food sold at the Hispanic Festival has become associated with national identity. *Pupusas* and tacos, for example, are reflective of Salvadoran and Mexican national identities. Pupusas, made from corn masa and commonly stuffed with cheese, beans, meat, or *loroco* (an edible flower from El Salvador) were unknown in the DC area before the 1980s. Although often sold along with the better-known Mexican foods, pupusas are today found in the food trucks that cruise the DC area, local markets, and numerous restaurants. (Left, courtesy of Olivia Cadaval; below, photograph by Michael Hoyt.)

Latino Youth Center and Centro de Arte members created the masks pictured above. El Centro de Arte was cofounded by Chilean Carlos Salazar, who, like many other South American artists, came to DC fleeing widespread political repression and violence. He designed a landmark mural in Adams Morgan titled *Un pueblo sin murales es un pueblo desmuralizado* ("A people without murals is a demuralized people"). (Photograph by Rick Reinhard.)

Murals became part of the identity of the neighborhoods, or *barrios*, in which they were painted. The murals also provide a sense of connection among Latinos because they portray various stories and a shared ethnic aesthetic. Many of the murals, particularly in the Adams Morgan area, have been lost due to gentrification and rebuilding. Here, a young artist contributes to a mural. Many murals were painted by students at the Latin American Youth Center. (Photograph by Rick Reinhard.)

In 1998, there were 450 Latino soccer teams in the metropolitan area. On page A1 in the *Washington Post*'s Sunday edition, November 29, 1998, Gabriel Escobar, a Washington Post staff writer, writes that "[t]he soccer spectacle has become the most visible manifestation of the Latino community at play, a sporting pageant staged every weekend on all the green space local governments can provide." Above, the local Peruvian soccer team, Somos Peru, poses for a picture. Below, the La Union team from Fairfax, Virginia, poses. (Both, courtesy of *El Pregonero*.)

Above, the Marco Antonio Etcheverry Soccer Academy members pose for a photograph. The academy was founded by the namesake and Bienvenido Martinez and Segundo Pezo, who worked in the business office of the Major League Soccer team DC United. Marco Antonio Etcheverry, a Bolivian soccer star known as "El Diablo," began playing with DC United in 1996. He told the *Washington Business Journal* reporters in 2002 that he "enjoy[s] teaching kids the game . . . but more than soccer, we want to teach them self-esteem and responsibility." Below, the Bolivian soccer team poses for a picture in 1992. (Both courtesy of *El Pregonero*.)

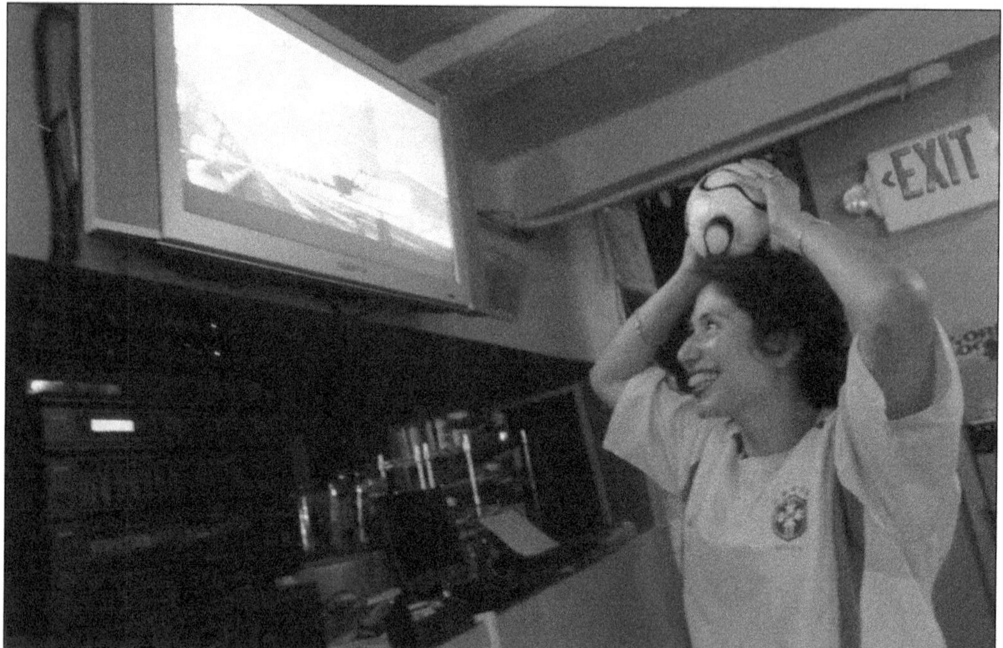

Watching soccer is an important pastime and often a ritualized event. Soccer is a shared cultural experience worldwide but particularly in the Americas. Here, a soccer fan of the Brazilian team watches the 2006 World Cup at a DC-area café. (Courtesy of *El Tiempo Latino*.)

Las Posadas (Nativity) was presented by GALA Theatre's youth group in Adams Morgan in 1980. Grupo de Artistas Latino Americanos (GALA) was founded by Hugo Medrano and his wife, Rebecca Read, in 1976. Like many other fellow artists and intellectuals, Medrano left his native Argentina during the military junta's "dirty war" against civilians. Many of those who settled in the DC area continued their artistic endeavors or sought positions in the academic community. (Photograph by Rick Reinhard.)

GALA's 2005 production of *Yerma*, written by the Spanish playwright Frederico Garcia Lorca, featured actors Ana Veronica Munoz (right) and Miriam Cruz. From its humble beginnings in a DC townhouse in 1976, the now full-fledged theater company, housed in the historic Tivoli Theater in Columbia Heights, is devoted to offering bilingual productions featuring US-Latino and Latin American playwrights. It is considered one of DC's cultural treasures. (Photograph by Daniel Cima; courtesy of GALA Theatre.)

Yepeto, by playwright Roberto Cossa, opened Teatro de la Luna's first season in 1990. Mario Marcel, the artistic director and founder of Teatro de la Luna (right), established this Hispanic theater company in 1991 with his Paraguayan wife, Nucky Walder, after arriving from his native Argentina in 1984. Teatro de la Luna is headquartered in Washington and has a venue at the Gunston Arts Center in Arlington, Virginia. At left is Carlos Ramirez, and at center is Claire Sharp. (Courtesy of Teatro de la Luna.)

From Teatro de la Luna's 1999–2000 season, *Cuentos de Hadas* (Fairy Tales) by Uruguyan playwright Raquel Diana featured young Venzuelan actress Anabel Marcano with Muriel Alfoneseca in the background. (Photograph by Daniel Cima; courtesy of Teatro de la Luna.)

Seen here in 2001, Quique Aviles, a noted local poet, actor, and activist, came to the Washington, DC, area in 1980 at age 15 from El Salvador. He established the LatiNegro Theater Collective, a grassroots theater group that highlighted the talents of young urban Latino and African American artists. His artistic works focus on the experiences of the marginalized. He serves as director of Gala Theatre's community-building youth initiative, Paso Nuevo. (Photograph by Rick Reinhard.)

Coral Cantigas is one of the few choral groups in the nation dedicated to presenting a dynamic mix of classical, folk, and popular music compositions for voice from the vast repertoire of Latin American, Caribbean, and Spanish music. The group has been performing in the Washington, DC, area for over 23 years. (Courtesy of Coral Cantigas.)

A native of Puerto Rico, Diana Saez, founder and director of Coral Cantigas, moved to the suburbs of Washington, DC, with her Chilean husband in the 1980s. She holds master's degrees from both Harvard University and Temple University. She received her doctoral degree in music from the University of Maryland and has been invited to serve as guest choral director all over the United States. (Courtesy of Coral Cantigas.)

Rosana Azar, left, an Argentine artist, immigrated with her family to United States in 1991 in search of an opportunity to develop her full potential as an artist. Since arriving in Silver Spring, Maryland, she has dedicated herself to her art, her two children, and directing the nonprofit Creative Adventures, an arts education program in 25 Montgomery County schools. Her artwork has been exhibited nationally and internationally. She invites viewers to immerse themselves on an exploration of color and dreams. Below is her painting *Self Knowledge*, an oil on canvas measuring 18 feet by 26 feet that was painted between 1990 and 1999. (Both, courtesy of Rosana Azar.)

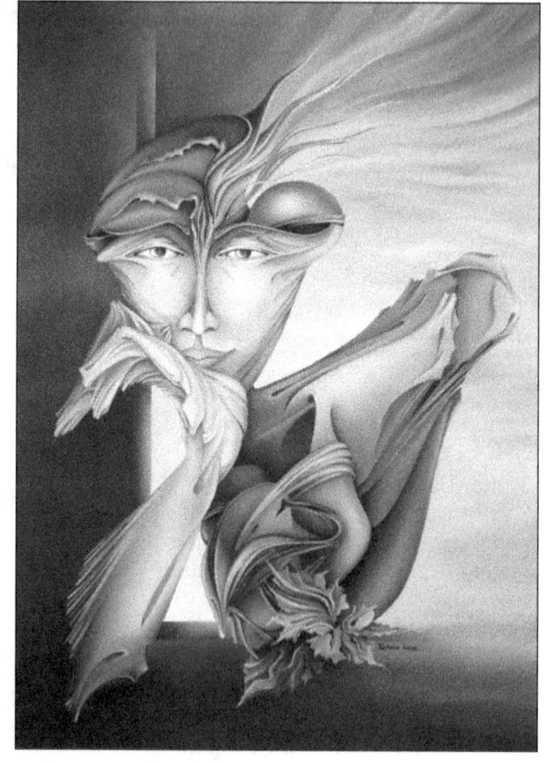

Nine

SPIRITUAL LIFE

"Everybody brought their own saint," reflected Teresa Wright, originally from Mexico, as she discussed the history of the Hispanic community in the Washington, DC, area.

Churches and temples in the United States have historically tended to the spiritual and the material needs of immigrants. They have served as clearinghouses for information on jobs, housing, economic opportunities, and education; provided food pantries and clothing outlets; and facilitated the adaptation of immigrants by offering English and citizenship preparation classes. They have also helped immigrants navigate the intricacies of government bureaucracies when seeking their services.

Unlike the Europeans and African Americans that preceded them, the majority of Latinos choosing the Washington, DC, metropolitan area as their final destination found it unnecessary to set in place the cornerstones of their places of worship. Upon their arrival in this area, they were confronted with a multiplicity of well-established religious denominations eagerly seeking their affiliation. This was especially true of Roman Catholics. The archdiocese of Washington claims a flock of over 620,000 Catholics today in Maryland and DC alone and offers services in Spanish in 30 churches. For those Latinos in the region who are not Catholic, there is a broad array of long-established Protestant churches eager to welcome them, such as the Presbyterian, Episcopalian, Lutheran, Baptist, and Pentecostal.

For Latinos seeking non-institutional outlets for their unique religious praxis, the alternative has been services in rented basements, school cafeterias, or storefronts. This trend has been more prevalent among Central American Christians, of whom nationwide only three percent are mainline Protestant and 22 percent are Evangelicals. They are responsible for the creation of a constellation of places of worship dotting cities and suburbs in the Washington, DC, metropolitan area.

In the mid-20th century, the Academy of American Franciscan History was established in Potomac, Maryland. Church masses were mostly conducted in Spanish for the international residents of Hispanic origin in the metropolitan area. The academy's chapel, shown here, was built in 1961 using the plans of a Peruvian architect, Harth Terre, and assembled with objects and art from Peru. In 1989, the academy moved to Berkeley, California, where it continues to publish the journal *The Americas: A Quarterly Review of Latin America.* It is unknown what became of the structure itself. (Courtesy of Maria Helena Malagón.)

In 1953, Padre Lino, from Galicia, Spain, a historian and a priest, presided over the first communion of Maria Helena Malagón, also a Spaniard. The service was held at the Academy of American Franciscan History, which at the time was located on Cedar Lane in Bethesda. In 1961, the academy moved to Potomac, Maryland. (Courtesy of Maria Helena Malagón.)

Jessica Martinez was born in Paraguay but was baptized in Maryland. Here she is in 1995 when she was nine months old; she is shown at her baptism at St. Catherine Laboure Catholic Church on Viers Mill Road in Wheaton, Maryland. The entire family attended the baptism. The godparents, Viviana Gaona and Chrispulo Gaona, are present. Jessica's mother, Oilda Gaona, is holding her as her father, Juan Carlos Martinez, looks on. At right is Jessica Martinez's first communion picture. The picture was taken in 2005 at the family home in Twinbrook, near Rockville, Maryland. The first communion ritual was held at St. Jude's Catholic Church. (Both, courtesy of Oilda Gaona.)

St. Martin's Church in Gaithersburg, Maryland, was an important place for fellowship among the Hispanics arriving in the early 1970s. By 1980, more than 25 people, mostly white-collar professionals from many Hispanic countries, attended the irregularly scheduled Spanish masses. Fr. David Brooks, shown here in August 1980, was the first Spanish-speaking priest at St. Martin's. From left to right are Lourdes Maria Gutierrez, Fr. Ron Smedley, Fr. David Brooks, and Ana Calderon Blanco. (Courtesy of Fr. David Brooks.)

One of the many various religions processions that take place in the streets of Washington, DC, is the Good Friday procession of the Catholic churches. This one proceeds along Connecticut Avenue near Eighteenth and M Streets in the 1980s. (Courtesy of Olivia Cadaval.)

In an annual October rite brought to DC by Peruvian immigrants, the Lord of Miracles Celebration (*La Hermandad del Senor de Los Milagros*) takes place in the Adams Morgan and Kalorama neighborhoods of Northwest Washington, DC. During the procession, which lasts most of the day, various performances, food, and religious rites occur. (Photograph by Michael Hoyt.)

Our Lady of Lujan is carried by members of the Argentinean military on May 21, 2007, at the Basilica of the National Shrine of the Immaculate Conception in Washington, DC. She is the patroness of Catholics in Argentina, Uruguay, and Paraguay. The tradition of celebrating a mass in honor of a patron saint or the Virgin Mary that is affiliated with a particular country continues among many of the Latino Catholics in the Washington, DC, area. (Courtesy of *El Pregonero*.)

The children of the Hispanic congregation at the Bethesda United Methodist Church in Bethesda, Maryland, reenact the Nativity during the 1999 Christmas season. Congregants of this church, many of whom were immigrants and did not have extended family in the area, would share a potluck Christmas supper following the service. The typical Christmas meal reflected the diversity of the congregation and included black beans and rice, roasted pork, *pasteles*, and flan. (Courtesy of Linda Robinson)

The women's group of the Hispanic congregation of Bethesda United Methodist Church celebrates a Christmas-season lunch with its pastor, the Cuban-born Rev. Yolanda Pupo-Ortiz, pictured in the middle of the row on the right. Reverend Pupo-Ortiz was the first Latina to be fully ordained by the New England Methodist Conference and has a long history of involvement in issues of social justice. (Courtesy of Linda Robinson.)

Ana Brito, pictured third from the left with her fellow church members and pastor of the Hispanic congregation of the Bethesda United Methodist Church, receives the 1994 Maryland Governor's Commission on Hispanic Affairs Public Service Award for the after-school tutoring program for Hispanic youth called Ayuda Especial. Many Hispanic churches initiated community service programs to help immigrants in the DC area. As of 2013, the program has helped countless Latino youth and their parents over its 25-year history. (Courtesy of Linda Robinson.)

With migration came the spread of Spanish-language evangelical churches. At a Spanish-language Jehovah's Witness church in Maryland, parishioners have come together to celebrate children. (Courtesy of Juana Gonzalez.)

Church signs throughout the metro area show the spread of Spanish-language services and churches as well as the different denominations followed by the Latino community. Most of Latinos in the United States are Roman Catholic. Only about five percent attend a mainstream Protestant church, but today the numbers are growing. At left, the United Spanish Methodist Church sign calls to parishioners along New Hampshire Avenue in Takoma Park, Maryland. The stretch of New Hampshire Avenue in Montgomery County has often been referred to as the "highway to heaven" because of the number and diversity of places of worship that are located there. (Both, courtesy of *El Pregonero*.)

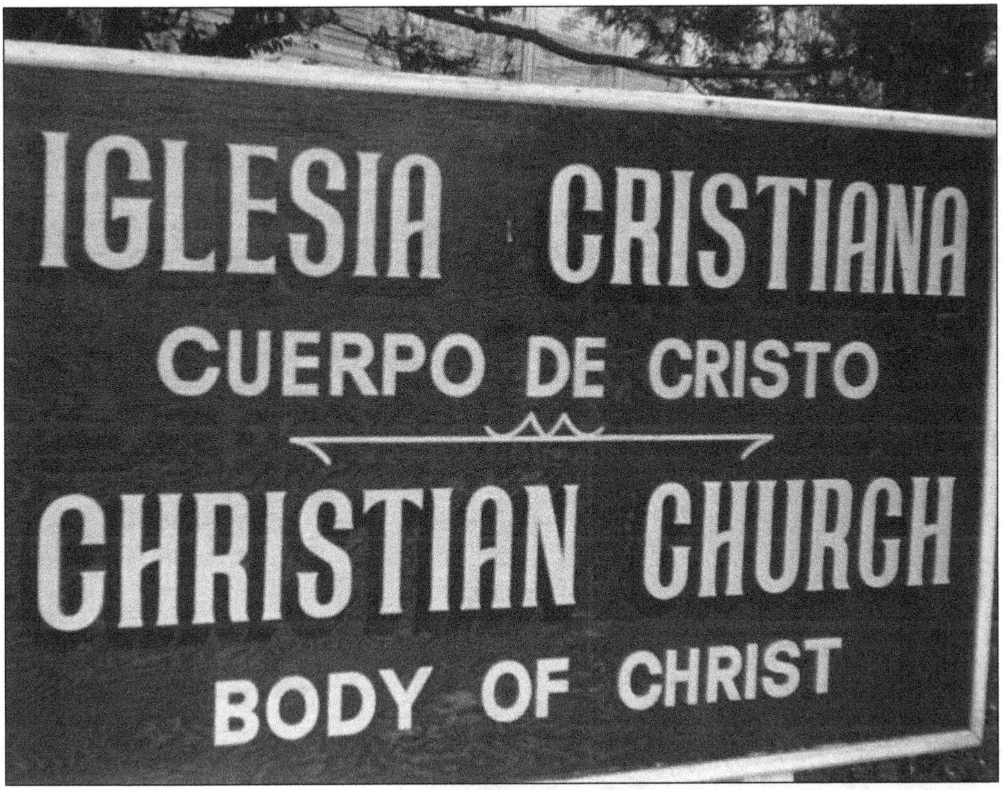

Above, date unknown, a sign announces the Body of Christ Church. At right, date unknown, the sign announces the Spanish Baptist Church at Columbia Road and Sixteenth Street, the heart of the early Latino barrio. (Both, courtesy of *El Pregonero.*)

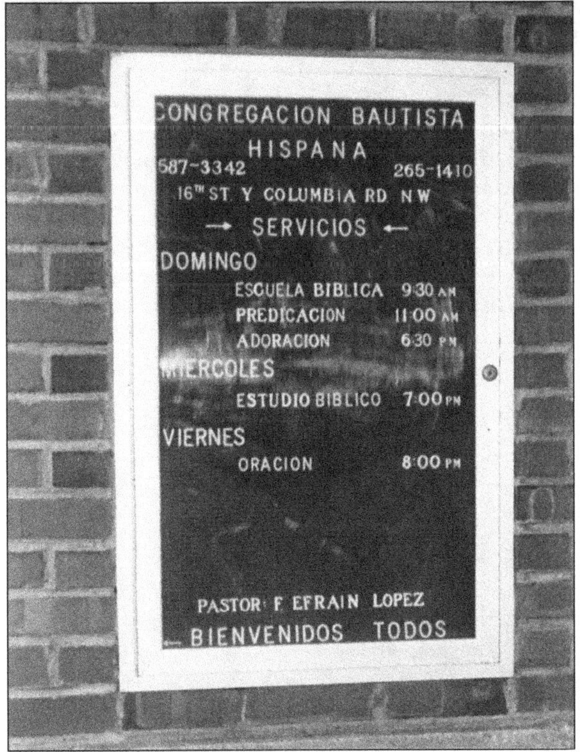

For many years Fr. Dalton Downs (right), originally from Corn Island, Nicaragua, served as the vice-chair of the Peace Commission, established by the Episcopal Diocese of Washington, to educate and support peace initiatives around the world, particularly in Africa and Latin America. On this night in Washington, DC, the commission recognized Archbishop Desmond Tutu (left) as the recipient of the Peace Commission Award for his outstanding work promoting and working for peace in South Africa. Father Downs's wife, Ana Jo Downs (center), a native of Puerto Rico, joined them. (Courtesy of Fr. Dalton Downs.)

Ten

LA FAMILIA

Although every family is unique and there are cultural differences among families from different Spanish-speaking countries, a common theme among Latino families is the value placed on family, or *la familia*. Of course, most people value family, and some place a greater emphasis on the degree of responsibility toward, expectations of, and power of the bonds of the family, a pattern notable in Latino culture. Latino families tend to be close-knit and the family is the most important social unit for all its members. The concept of family reaches beyond the nuclear family set of parents and children to include grandparents, aunts, uncles, cousins, godparents, and often close friends. As a consequence, Latino families and households overall tend to be larger than other groups. The good of the family is often placed above the need of the individual. Family members often feel a strong responsibility for each other and support each other in times of crisis and during significant life events.

Many Latinos have migrated to the Washington area to be with family. Strong family ties have caused others to stay in the area to be near their families. It is not atypical for children to live with their families well into adulthood; and once they move, they tend to stay in close proximity to their family. Thus, many first-, second-, and third-generation Hispanics have remained in the area and close to their families—a dynamic that has created groupings of Latinos who have ties to the same country. Latinos typically prefer to engage in activities that include their children. It is not unusual, therefore, for all types of social functions and events to be multigenerational. It is with the family that Latinos celebrate Sunday barbecues, soccer matches, and the many rites of passage of life, including baptisms, birthdays, weddings, and anniversaries.

A Salvadoran family relaxes on a Sunday morning in Washington, DC, in 1984. Not all Salvadoran families enjoyed a scene like this in the 1980s and 1990s. Many families were separated by the civil war, ensuing social strife, and conditions of immigration. (Photograph by Rick Reinhard.)

Alba Robinson-Contreras is sightseeing in Washington, DC, in 1969 with a friend, Anita Brito, who has recently arrived from Cuba. The Brito family came to the Washington area as refugees sponsored by the United Methodist Church. Alba, a native of Puerto Rico and member of a local Methodist congregation, helped the newly arrived Brito family settle into their new home in the suburbs of Maryland. (Courtesy of Linda Robinson.)

Alba celebrates her birthday with family and friends in her home in Aspen Hill. In 1965, when Alba arrived with her American husband, there were very few Hispanic families living in her Aspen Hill–area neighborhood. The few Hispanics living in the easternmost suburbs of Montgomery County, Maryland, met each other by word of mouth, and many formed lifelong friendships and informal networks that helped newcomers make the transition to life in the States. (Courtesy of Linda Robinson.)

This image shows Alba Robinson Contreras standing while 11-year-old Julia Rueda, daughter of a Mexican diplomat stationed in Washington, DC, is seated next to her along with Alba's daughter, Linda, at a social get-together in the Ruedas' home in Rockville, Maryland, 1970. (Courtesy of Linda Robinson.)

Linda Robinson Contreras hangs up a doll piñata at her birthday party in March 1969. Piñatas were rare in those days and had to be handmade or purchased in one of the few stores that sold Latino products in the Adams Morgan and Mount Pleasant areas of DC. (Courtesy of Linda Robinson.)

Javier Malagón enjoys playtime with his two granddaughters Lisa (left) and Maria at his home in Bethesda, Maryland, in 1969. Exiled from Spain because of the civil war, he and his wife, Helena Perenya Malagón, had always planned to return to Spain. The main reason they stayed in the DC area was to be close to their daughter and granddaughters. (Courtesy of Maria Helena Malagón.)

Through the IDB, the Dominguez family made close friendships with other Paraguayan families. They celebrated holidays and family events and vacationed together at many locations, including Ocean City, Maryland. At their parties they would have *asados* (barbecue) and other typical Paraguayan foods, listen to Paraguayan music, and, of course, dance. (Courtesy of Marty Dominguez.)

In this 1960s image, the Dominguez family poses in traditional dress. From left to right stand Marty, Celia Ruiz, and Chely. Dr. Raimund Dominguez (missing in the picture) came to the United States and worked as an economist at the Inter-American Development Bank (IDB). They lived in Potomac, Maryland, where they continued to celebrate Paraguayan culture with a close-knit group of Maryland Paraguayans. Today, Marty Dominguez lives in DC and is the director of marketing for C-SPAN. (Courtesy of Marty Dominguez.)

At right, Carolina Wright poses in a Spanish dress, and below, Elizabeth Wright poses in a Mexican dress from Tehuantepec on the lawn of their childhood home in Montgomery Village, Maryland, in 1971. Both girls were born in the United States, but their mother, Teresa Wright, was born in Mexico. The girls and their other siblings were raised bilingual and bicultural during a time when few Hispanic families lived in the Gaithersburg area. Today, Carolyn is a manager at Identity, a community-based organization that works with Latino youth and families in Montgomery County. Elizabeth is a professor of Spanish at the University of Georgia whose work requires her to travel often to Spain. (Both, courtesy of the Wright Family.)

The Wrights are seated in their Montgomery Village, Maryland, home in 1981. From left to right are Carolyn; Inge Van Eynde, an exchange student; Teresa; Elizabeth; and grandmother Esperanza Rios. Teresa Wright, originally from Mexico, recalls moving to Montgomery Village in 1971 when there were only five Spanish-speaking families in the village. They soon made a tight-knit group of friends from various countries in Latin America. (Courtesy of the Wright family.)

Dr. Emma Violand-Sánchez poses with her daughter, Julia, and her son, James. This photograph was taken around 1989. Following in their mother's footsteps, today both Julia and James are educators. (Courtesy of Emma Violand-Sánchez.)

In August 1980, Emma Violand-Sánchez poses with her mother and five sisters. From left to right are Ana Elisabeth, Susana, Julia, mother Emma Sánchez, Maria Eugenia, Emma, and Patricia. The family is originally from Cochabamba, in central Bolivia. Emma Violand-Sánchez came to Virginia in 1961 when she was in high school. In an interview with David Bearinger of the Virginia Foundation for the Humanities, she reflects on her past: "My father had been exiled for organizing against the government. I was one of six daughters, and my mother couldn't support all of us in Bolivia. I had an aunt who was living in the United States at the time, and so it was decided that the three oldest girls—I was the second—would come here. I was to live with an American family and attend school. The quota for visas for immigrants from Latin America had just been raised, and sponsorships were available. My parents made the decision, and that was that." (Courtesy of Emma Violand-Sánchez.)

Celebrations that involve family and friends are an important part of Latino life. Above, the family of Juana Gonzalez celebrates the birthdays of her children—Pablo, Sara, and Ana—in Wheaton Regional Park, a popular location for parties and outdoor play for many local families. This particular party took place in 1986. Joining in on the celebration are friends who were originally from China, Colombia, and Cuba. At left, Juana Gonzalez and her family play in the snow. Juana Gonzalez immigrated to the United States from Canton La Estancia, Cacaopera, El Salvador, in 1978. For a time, she was separated from her three children, who remained in El Salvador. They were reunited in the United States, where they formed an even larger family with their US-born siblings, Juan Carlos and Angelica. (Both, courtesy of Juana Gonzalez.)

When Juana Gonzalez's daughter Ana turned 15, the family celebrated with a *quinceañera*—the traditional and often elaborate 15th birthday celebration for girls in many Hispanic cultures. Above, Ana poses with her father and mother. Below, two children in the court of honor pose before the celebration. The court of honor in a quinceañera is made up of a group of siblings, friends, and cousins that the celebrant chooses to share the spotlight with her. During the quinceañera party, the court performs a choreographed dance with the quinceañera. (Both, courtesy of Juana Gonzalez.)

Xiomarra Blanco celebrates her 15th birthday party, or quinceañera, in Washington, DC, in May 1991. In many Latin American cultures, families celebrate the 15th birthdays of their daughters. Quinceañeras are large, and often elaborate, events that involve much preparation. While some are religious in nature and involve a religious service, others are completely secular. (Photograph by Rick Reinhard.)

On January 10, 2004, Jessica Martinez, originally from Paraguay, celebrated her ninth birthday at Jeepers in Rockville, Maryland. Jeepers is no longer in business in Rockville, but at the time it provided loads of fun for children and even incorporated piñatas into the parties. Piñatas are birthday traditions in Hispanic culture. (Courtesy of Oilda Gaona.)

A traditional family playground for Washington metro area families is Ocean City, Maryland, where the extended Martinez Gaona family would go for summer vacations. The Martinez Gaona family immigrated to the United States from Paraguay beginning in the 1970s, when political turmoil became increasingly worse under the dictatorship of Alfredo Stroessner, whose dictatorship ended in 1989. Shown in the above picture are, from left to right, (first row) Carlos Martinez, Oilda Gaona, Guillermina Gaona, and Ismelda Gaona; (second row) Jessica Martinez, Fabiana Gaona, and Bridget O'Harrah (a school friend). Posing on the beach in the image below are, from left to right, Bridget O'Harrah, Jessica Martinez, and Fabiana Gaona. (Both, courtesy of Oilda Gaona.)

The Butler family was born in 1994 in Managua, Nicaragua, when Malcolm and Tish adopted baby brothers Martin and Tony and brought them to McLean, Virginia. The family also lived in Guatemala (1996–1999) and traveled to Mexico, Belize, Costa Rica, and the Dominican Republic. The "boys" (now 21 and 20) have grown up in Fairfax County, Virginia, where they now reside and work. They remain fully conscious of their Latino heritage, which has been happily melded into their large Anglo-Irish extended family. From left to right are Martin, Letitia Kelly, Malcolm, and Anthony Butler. (Photograph by Philip Bermingham Photography.)

Bibliography

American Latino Heritage Projects. National Park Service. Accessed August 15, 2013. http://www.nps.gov/latino/

Cadaval, Olivia. "The Latino Community: Creating an Identity in the nation's capital". *Urban Odyssey: A Multicultural History of Washington DC*. Washington, DC: Smithsonian Institution Press, 1996: 231–249.

———. *Creating a Latino Identity in the Nation's Capital: The Latino Festival*. New York and London: Garland Publishing, Inc., 1998.

Comey, Jennifer et al. *State of Latinos in the District of Columbia*. Urban Institute Policy Center. November 2009. http://www.urban.org/UploadedPDF/412176-state-of-latinos.pdf

Escobar, Gabriel. "The Other Pro Soccer." The *Washington Post*, November 29, 1998, sec. A1.

Fernandez-Shaw, Carlos M. *Presencia Española en los Estados Unidos*. Madrid: Ediciones Cultura Hispanica, 1972.

Grymes, Charles A. *The Spanish in Virginia before Jamestown*. Accessed August 15, 2013. http://www.virginiaplaces.org/settleland/spanish.html

Johnson, Etta. *A New American Community of Learners in Arlington, Virginia*. Seattle: CreateSpace, 2013.

Lopez, Mark Hugo and Daniel Dockterman. "A Growing and Diverse Population: Latinos in the Washington, DC, Metropolitan Area." *Hispanic Migration and Urban Development: Studies from Washington DC*. Bingley, UK: Emerald Group Publishing Limited, 2012: 83–110.

Maryland Department of Legislative Services. Office of Policy Analysis. *Overview of Hispanic Community in Maryland*. Annapolis, 2008.

Peña, Elaine. Latino D.C. *History Project: Synopsis and Prototype Case Study Phase I (2009–2010)*. Smithsonian Latino Center. Accessed August 15, 2013. http://www.latino.si.edu/PDF/Phase_1_Latino_DC_History_Project_PENA.pdf

Pumar, Enrique. *Hispanic Migration and Urban Development: Studies from Washington DC*. Bingley, UK: Emerald Group Publishing Limited, 2012.

Ready, Timothy. *Latino Immigrant Youth: Passages from Adolescence to Adulthood*. New York and London: Garland Publishing, Inc., 1991.

Repak, Terry. *Waiting on Washington: Central American Workers in the Nation's Capital*. Philadelphia: Temple University Press, 1995.

Suárez-Orozco, Marcelo and Mariela Páez. *Latinos Remaking America*. Berkeley: University of California Press, 2009.

www.ingramcontent.com/pod-product-compliance
Lightning Source LLC
LaVergne TN
LVHW081546100826
845153LV00004B/322

* 9 7 8 1 5 3 1 6 7 3 2 2 2 *